D0000683

Victorian Furniture

OUR AMERICAN HERITAGE

BOOK II

KATHRYN McNERNEY

COLLECTOR BOOKS

A Division of Schroeder Publishing Co., Inc.

The current values of this book should be used only as a guide. They are not intended to set prices, which vary from one section of the country to another. Auction prices as well as dealer prices vary and are affected by condition as well as demand. Neither the Author nor the Publisher assumes responsibility for any losses that might be incurred as a result of consulting this guide.

Cover Photo: Courtesy of Bob and Harriet Swedberg, *Collector's Encyclopedia of American Furniture, Volume I*. Walnut marble top commode washstand, 28"w x 16"dp x 24"h x 12" splash back. $800.00.

Searching For A Publisher?

We are always looking for knowledgeable people considered to be experts within their fields. If you feel that there is a real need for a book on your collectible subject and have a large comprehensive collection, contact us.

COLLECTOR BOOKS
P.O. Box 3009
Paducah, Kentucky 42002-3009

Cover design by Beth Summers
Book design by Gina Lage

Printed by IMAGE GRAPHICS, INC., Paducah, Kentucky

DEDICATION

As the book grew I'd often pause to phone one or both for a "listening" audience ever ready to reply...and so...for always may these pages hold memories for "Kindred Spirits"...my two dear daughters.

SHARON KATHRYN FISHER
MARTHA ANN LANE McNERNEY

APPRECIATION

Not only did each of you and many others share with me your knowledge of antiques and collectibles, but you also permitted photography of your furniture treasures...and beyond those courtesies I could not forget your friendliness. I am grateful.

Florida	Fernandina Beach	Amelia Antique Market
		Eight Flags Antique Mall
		Rosanna Oliver
	Jacksonville	Avondale Antique Mall
		The Lamp Post Antiques, Inc.
	Jacksonville Beach	Beaches Antique Gallery
	Mandarin	Bayard Country Store
		Maryanne Bratburd
	Middleburg	Carolyn Lane
		The Tom McNerneys
	Orange Park	B & D Antiques
		Ladybug Antiques and Collectables
		Mr. and Mrs. Robert George
		The David Bells
		Timely Treasures Antiques
	Pensacola	Robert and Lorene Rodgers
Georgia	Cave Spring	Country Roads Antique Mall
	Rome	Steve and Joan Fellows
		Ozment Antique Gallery
New York	Clarence	Exhibitors at Clarence Antique World and Exposition
		Ruth's Antiques, Inc.
		The Mule Skinner
	Lewiston	Lexington Square
		Museum, Plain & Niagara Sts.
		Stimson's Antiques & Gifts
	Lockport	Exhibitors at A Festival of Antiques, Keenan Center
	Ransomville	Wayne and Audrey Orr
	Towers Corners	Town Hall, Town of Porter
	Youngstown	Lucile Bennett
		Kathy Goller
		Mr. and Mrs. Howard Tower
		Mr. and Mrs. Richard Smithson
		Nettie Martin
		Pat McCaw
		Sharon Fisher
Ohio	St. Paris	Mr. and Mrs. Jacob L. Arnold

CONTENTS

ABBREVIATIONS

bk	back
ca	circa, around the time of, about
dia	diameter
dp	depth
fl	height from the floor
frt	front
h	height
l	length, long
NP	no price — museum property
pr	pair
rd	round
ref	refinished
repro	reproductions
res	restoration
t	tall
w	width

◆◆◆◆◆◆◆◆◆

This is the author's report, not appraisals, of furniture shown herein. Values are according to price tags in the marketplaces; values for prices in private collections are set by the owners.

◆◆◆◆◆◆◆◆◆

For dealers, many factors must be considered before tags are written. While recognizing universally acclaimed worth of true antiques and collectibles, all must be weighed, such as present trend of buyers' interests, regional economies, travel costs to find stocks, the age, condition, rarity, signatures or touch-marks or dates on pieces, and a reasonable profit to stay in business. And now...as you turn the pages...may you enjoy the book!

DISTINCTIVELY VICTORIAN

Furniture, properly defined as "movable objects (chests, stools, beds, tables, and such), was for equipping rooms. In Victorian style, bare spaces between, in, on, and over them were filled with statuary, curtains, carpets, bric-a-brac, etc., all included under the word "furniture." Although today, in our way of classifying everything into separate niches we would call them "furnishings," herein they are contained as first intended ..."furniture."

No pictures are duplicated from Book I, *Victorian Furniture, Our American Heritage*. In the preponderance of factory-made pieces there could be "look alikes" and "similars." But even several from the same productions, made over identical patterns, in that burgeoning nineteenth century could under close scrutiny reveal infinitesimal differences. Unless stated, mirrors are in fine condition with beveled edges. Surface refinishing, when needed, has been professionally done to the originals, all objects now shown in fine or mint condition. Restorations are indicated; where extensive repairs and/or replacement parts are imperative, in most cases those articles were so-tagged in the shops; also noted on the following pages. In such cases, shop sales were usually made "as is."

When the first permanent settlers reached our shores, for the majority, the realities of survival were paramount. Little energy was left at the end of each day to plan anything beyond the morrow's labors. They plodded along, until increased incomes, time and leisure afforded by tremendous technical innovations in industries activated the restless ambitions of our intriguing 1800's. And as it has been since time immemorial, their furniture paralleled each step of their cultural development.

For a while, cabinetmakers owning their own shops or employed by others attracted customers profitably. Their themes recalled those of ancient Rome, Greece, Persia, and Egypt, incorporating such early lines into what they themselves evolved. Sometimes they applied the patterns of one, more often they combined ideas of several much earlier makers. The results were the "Revival" styles of Victoriana. And although gradually absorbed into the more dominant factories, now and then skilled craftsmen were given the responsibility of the handcrafting on "special orders."

Manufacturers lost no hours reflecting on what had been...they just copied what they wanted from the past, using the old along with their own conceptions of the "Revivals." When considering specific classifications "eclectic" seems the term most apropos along with "loosely applied" or "covering many different makers' interpretations." Substyle and transitional are two other identifications, the first meaning "below the original," and latter meaning "flowing from one stage of development to another."

Faced with the prospect of an easier way to earn their living, folks rushed from rural districts to the centers of industries. Due to the heady influence of the need for real (or pseudo) importance, people went on frantically impetuous buying sprees to stuff their rooms with every bit of furniture they could possibly squeeze in. Quality was not half so desirable as number of pieces, heavy ornamentation and "keeping up with the Jones's" or surpassing them. Even during the shortages brought about by the Civil War, many northern factories kept running full blast turning out innumerable pieces, scarcely able to fill orders. And quality, in most cases, was very good. New "assembly line" methods increased output. However, there were limits to the heights of decorating, and one day, many pieces reached the grotesque in garish ornamentation.

The growth of a new middle class occurred simultaneously with all the improved and newly invented machine processes. Unaccustomed affluence gave the newcomers an exhilarating sense of wellbeing so when they saw what they wanted they bought it, not bothering to look at price tags. But somehow, deep down remained a glimmer of that generations-instilled conformity (publicly, at least) to social restrictions. Among the "things" remembered...my country Granny said, "While you're worrying about what somebody else thinks about how you look, they probably aren't even thinking about you...just be careful how you act!" In 1837 when England's young Queen Victoria began her reign, proper deportment (observed as strictly on this side of the Atlantic) and the need to keep up appearances were moral imperatives!

While embracing every new furniture phase that came along, Victorians eventually found their acquisitional appetites cloyed with "too much of enough." Although they were hesitant to suddenly accept a "new look," the French delicacies, ponderous Empire, and the Gothics, among others, were gradually subsiding, as with the transition of Rococo into the lesser pretentiousness of Louis XVI. But the inevitable step toward leaving massiveness and effusiveness in their furniture evolved during late Victoriana, for then appeared the Arts and Crafts Movement, Art Nouveau, Charles Locke Eastlake of Britain with his pronouncements of Good Taste, and the Stickley Brothers (Gustav for one) with their lines of Mission furniture.

Book I details the nineteenth century Revival Periods, giving makers and their works. To avoid repetition, following is a brief outline of that:

Under Early Victorian 1820 – 1850
　　Gothic Revival 1815 – 1880...crested in the 1840's
　　Rococo (Louis XV) Revival 1840 – 1870
　　Elusive Elizabethan Revival 1840 – 1850
　　Spool Turner 1815, advancing by 1830, large quantities made
　　　　1850 – 1860, reducing to small numbers by 1880; by the
　　　　1840's spool turnings had become so popular that some
　　　　factories made and sold only turnings to large factories
　　　　and cabinetmakers.
Cottage Style 1845 – 1900

Under Late Victorian 1850 – 1900
　　Renaissance Revival 1855 – 1880
　　Louis XVI Revival 1865 – 1880
　　Jacobean Revival 1870's

Early Americans used native woods as pine, maple, and cherry with some poplar and birch, adapting to utilitarian purposes then-current styles from England and other homelands. Expert cabinetmakers such as John Goddard and Duncan Phyfe added walnut and mahogany. More formal rosewood was a favorite with John Henry Belter when working on his magnificent Rococo Revival creations. Country makers were slow to imitate city fashions in furniture and for many years retained their own patterns (many similar to Colonial Revivals), using their sometimes inherited tools. With Cottage styles becoming prominent, much was painted and/or gilded; a Boston firm, Merrian & Parsons, specialized in making, advertising, and shipping "Cottage Chamber Furniture" and a whole line, such as bureaus, wardrobes, chairs, etc., from coast to coast. In later Victoriana, golden oak reached a pinnacle of demand, especially when heavily decorated. It retreated, as it had done in other years of its ups and downs, under the onslaught of Mission furniture. Today's shoppers for quality oak, walnut, and mahogany, particularly, can still find really fine examples available in the marketplaces.

Nevertheless, under increased recognition of the value and practicality, as well as the beauty of so much of Victoriana's furniture, this awareness will eventually deplete desirable stocks — and prices are bound to escalate even further. One well-known Florida dealer is having numerous calls for the brown-stained oaks, although still selling golden oak (the reputed "dust-deterrent" wood). A regular customer who heretofore had always furnished rooms only in mahogany was toying with the idea of adding one of the rarities in oak as an accent piece. A painted, false-grained wood, or handsomely inlaid table, for instance, will often pick up and accentuate the darker glowing tone of traditional walnut or the "good fire" of mahogany Empire Revival woods. Delicately regal styles, while somewhat less comfortable for relaxing, do charm the eyes, while the luxurious cushioning of Moorish and Turkish styles welcome and deeply embrace their occupants. The appealing pine, especially if it carries the age-earned satiny patina, even when placed among a dining room's or entry's more formal decor, is an eloquent spark of heritage — and a great conversational ice-breaker! In warm weather particularly, the light and airy woven rushes such as wicker and bamboo (the latter of natural bamboo or maple woods treated with turnings and dark-stained rings to imitate it) are cooling even to view.

Architects and their builders and furniture manufacturers many times borrowed ideas from each other. Architectural designers who were trying to depict characteristics from the Middle Ages found their "points and turrets for castles and cottages" incorporated in furniture and, in turn, architects used patterns from furniture, as stick and ball and other lengths and turnings among them, on and inside their buildings. (Often seen are the designs from Gothic Revival and the Rococo embellishments.)

Ah, the Victorians! And their incomparable furniture! To speak of one is to recall the other. None of our centuries in America surpasses the nineteenth, so colorful and fascinating in its entirety. It made vast contributions of new inventions, scientific discoveries, and progressive changes and improvements to existing production methods. Learning to standardize sizes of furniture intended for shipping resulted in easier handling and less expensive delivery. Mail order houses made home orders possible and until the last quarter of the 1800's, the richness of furniture paralleled the extremes in clothing fashions (don't forget those huge cartwheel hats loaded with fruits, flowers, feathers, ribbons, veiling and more!).

And, finally, on turning these pages for our second journey into the romantic world of Victorian furniture to see some of the pieces that have endured among the many that were made...remembering back...these help to envision...how it was!

PURCHASE YOUR
CLOTHING,
DRY GOODS,
CARPETS,
CLOAKS,
Gents' Furnishings,
Hats and Shoes
—AT—
BRONNERS?
404, 406, 408, 410, 412, 414,
416 and 418
MAIN STREET

UP THE WALK, THROUGH THE DOOR

Typical of one American Victorian architectural style, especially popular in our northern and mid-western regions is this home in which some of the furniture styles on the following pages may still abide. Built well over a hundred years ago in a small town. Noteworthy are the dark shutters (long ago always tightly closed and locked at eventide to keep out the unhealthy night air), the bulged-out columns, stick and ball and other turnings, Pennsylvania Dutch tulips atop posts, narrow windows at each doorside, a fanlight, and the inimitable wrap-around porch. The dwelling is an excellent example of furniture makers' and architects' related themes. After a pause in the hallway, our journey is resumed into the following pages, and we are better able to place the furniture pieces into imaginary rooms after having seen this truly Victorian home (still occupied).

HALL TREE
Ca. 1860; top section is carved from 1 pc. of
1¼" thick walnut, 32" at its widest dimension; mortised into the base, which is reinforced at the back to hold the upright
from tipping. Delicate fretwork in a medley of floral, bellflowers, and heart
designs; high pediment; uncommon brass
double knob-end hat and light garment
hooks (1 repaired) and wooden side holders for gentlemen's "sticks" and ladies'
parasols, and umbrellas, their tips to rest
in a cast iron drip pan in a Rococo Revival
style with its strongly embossed combined
shell and leafy-stemmed flowers (a motif
favored by various Philadelphia makers
from the pre-1840's far into the Victorian
years). Blocks and lines edge the iron
which is shaped to correspond with the
contours of the base and depression into
which the pan fits. 76"h. $795.00.

HALL TREE

Wood painted cream and pale blue, restored. Brass touches; painted iron drip pan with elaborate embossings to correspond with patterns on the top and crest; spool turnings; oval mirror. A look of the French influenced Rococo Revival with symmetrical fretwork patterns — and carrying on into the Cottage style of painting woods. 83"h x 24"w. $550.00.

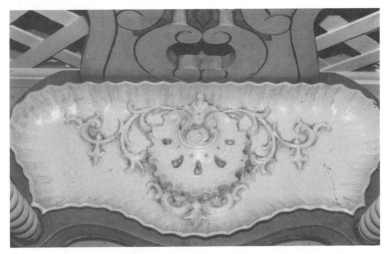

FLOOR FIRE SCREEN
Walnut frame having darkened reeding and molding on crest with a broken fleur-de-lis pediment. Center screen is silk of gold and silver threads; brilliants (resembling sequins) enhance an Oriental motif of peacocks, mosques, and colorful florals. 50½"h x 22"w. $395.00.

Although Oriental styles were noticed before the 1876 Centennial International Exhibition, those displays accelerated to incredible heights the fascination with Oriental patterns during the 1880's and 1890's.

FLOOR FIRE SCREEN

Extra-fine wire mesh with solid brass ornamentation on the wire and in framing; horn patterned handle for moving about; heavy brass "horseshoes" feet. These could be moved to shield against too much fireplace heat or window-glare from the sun. 28"h x 38"w. Georgia found. $450.00.

"SUMMER" FLOOR SCREEN

Ca. 1880; walnut with a center French style cloth-painted scenic of a troubadour and ladies; ball finials; reeded uprights; stick and ball spindles; shoe-feet on casters; (center framing as panels could be mounted inside or on a supporting frame). Seen on the Niagara Frontier. 35"h x 23"w. $165.00.

In summer, an idle fireplace could be hidden with one of these screens standing in front of it — sometimes homemakers add potted plants in front of the screen.

**SCREEN —
"GRATE" COVER**
Pure Victorian;
type usually set in
front of small fire-
places in parlors
and bedrooms that
burned coal (note
blackened under-
side from years of
usage). Copper and
iron; a winged
heart stamped
with dots from the
inside out; graceful
leaf handle, base
and legs of iron.
Pewter teapot sits
on a shelf on which
it could be kept
warm with the
cover placed close
enough — but not
so close as to burn.
28"h x 23"w, center
8" dp. $450.00.
(Pewter teapot val-
ued at $175.00 is
etched: "Harper's
Cold Tea.")

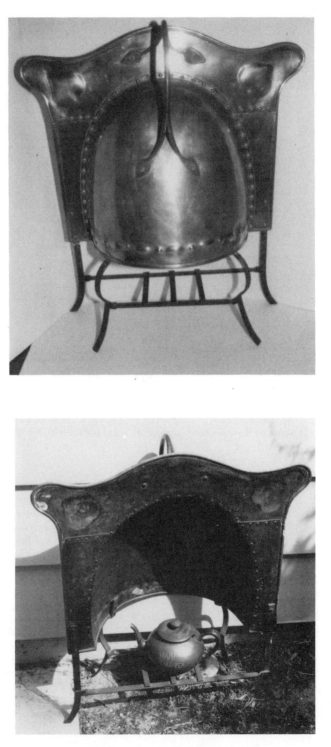

FRAME FOR THE FRONT OF A FIREPLACE
Origin an Atlanta, Georgia, estate sale; brass-faced iron case with
a liftout section; swellfront top piece; heavily embellished with
bowknots, (ice cream cone spindles?), scrolls, reeded columns,
urns of flowers, and draperies among them. 31"h x 26"w. $145.00.

ANDIRONS
Cast iron; each a detailed
woman's head and bust with
flame-shaped hair and wide
shoulders; all atop a reeded
column supported by horns of
plenty, a laurel wreath, and
four dog's feet (two at rear are
splayed) on a heavily patterned base. Victorian love of
elegance is everywhere about
the rooms, abundantly dis-
played even on the floor in this
handsome pair with the plain
long horizontal bars attached
at back to hold the logs. 13"h x
7"w. $125.00 pr.

FIREPLACE COAL BOX

Ornamental and practical in mahogany and brass; thick rolled sheet tin liftout basket for the coal. Basket can be removed by using the strong wire handle, bringing it through the outer long hinged side door. An embellished carrying bar at the top; a short wood-handled heavy tin scoop could be stored by slipping it through the iron bar at the rear side. 13¾"h x 13"w, top ledge 7¼"dp. $375.00.

PARLOR STOVE
No. 19 Rose Garland E model; mica door liner; elegantly embossed cast iron in varied patterns; nickel plated tall urn finial to lift off top; legs are removable. This one was used as a wood burner in a midwestern home. Without urn finial 37½"h. $235.00.

PARLOR STOVE
Black and nickel plating; embossed maker's label: Lawrence Stove Mfg. Co., Buffalo, N.Y.; mica liner on scroll-patterned base door with an opening bar to lift out that section for ash removal. 32"h x top oval 11"w x 7½"dp. $85.00.

PARLOR STOVE

Cast and sheet iron with nickel plating; removable legs; originally a gas heater, converted to coal and wood burner; placed on a brick platform in a lakeside Ontario home — stove pipe replaced to the original. 36"h, base 24"w x 12"dp. $350.00.

PARLOR STOVE

Ornate cast iron from a Belgian type; top lifts off using mushroom finial; two doors open at center; toward the end of the 1800's after central heating came to be, these stoves were used as auxiliary heaters to save money, to heat rooms not in the general heating plans (such as parlors that were only opened for special occasions) or to just "take off the chill" when dampness crept in. Inside parts are complete for usage. 37"h to top of finial x 15"dia base x 12"dia top. $250.00.

DOUBLE BED
Ca. 1870; walnut with finest burl inlays; Eastlake style (but can't escape elegance, at least in materials); follows a medley of patterns which portray tastes and habits of Victorian cabinetmakers and factories and their customers — borrowing from one or more styles in whatever piece they were making to their own ideas. 92"h x 78"l x 63"w. $1,700.00 up.

DOUBLE BED
Brass; cannonball finials; mushroom feet rest on iron casters; fancy decor. Mail order houses offered brass and iron beds. 54"h headboard x 42"w head and footboard. $800.00 up.

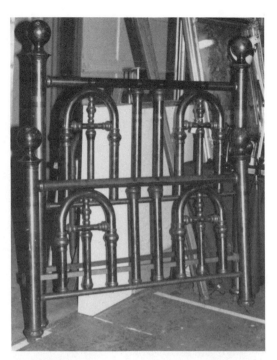

DOUBLE BED MADE INTO QUEEN SIZE
Black iron with brass ball finials and rosette trims. 59"h x 55½"w. $795.00 up.

Sears Roebuck 1897 catalog offered a brass trimmed iron bed much plainer than this one for $8.50, no charge for casters.

DOUBLE BED
Variable walnut; Eastlake style; subtle elegance in its simplicity of lines; burl center on panel top and footboards; grooves and incisings; reeded posts, horizontal column-like crest ends holding oblong curved design. It's easy to have slats to hold the mattress cut for these early beds from which the originals are almost always long gone. 73"h x 58"w x 78"l. $795.00.

DOUBLE BED
Poplar, walnut stained; complete with original side rails; applied 6"dia horizontal roll at headboard and one at the foot; vertical half rolls each with inverted base finial and rings; centers of both ends have upper half applied portion of a feathered fan; the crest of the headboard consists of applied moldings, half-ball and feather center-curve trims with a matching highpoint. An uncommon type of decorating. Headboard — 84"h x 59"w. Footboard — 39"h x 59"w. $895.00.

FOLDING (MURPHY) BED
Ca. 1880's; chestnut; ref.;
rare single bed size; brass
fixtures; pulls out and
down for sleeping position;
the inside springs are
showing considerable wear
and some rust — can still
hold a mattress but should
be replaced. 60"h x 31"w x
18"dp. $1,575.00.

BEDROOM SET, 3 Pcs

Called a Set, Suite, or Suit, pronounced "sweet" or just "suit." Serpentine lines; solid cherry; applied delicate embellishments along with flutings, and brass fixtures; all drawer sides and bottoms are made from oak wood, their front corners dovetailed, and the corners at back mortised. All drawer escutcheons are of the same design, but drawer pulls on the washstand/commode differ from those on the bureau. The shield framed mirror is held by wishbone uprights whose tops are cornucopias containing fancy brass fasteners that permit the mirror to tilt. $2,195.00.

Double Bed — 72" headboard x 35"h footboard. Bed is 56"w and 77"l.

Bureau — chest is 33"h x 47½"w x 22½"dp. Mirror is 36"h with a 1"w bevel.

Washstand/Commode — 30"h x 36½"w x 19"dp.

SINGLE BED
Cottage style in mahogany; long iron bolts originally held the cross boards at top and bottom of bed — the holes where they were installed are very evident but the bolts are missing; turnings, curves, and casters. Headboard — 32"h x 39"w. Footboard — 22"h x 39"w. $275.00.

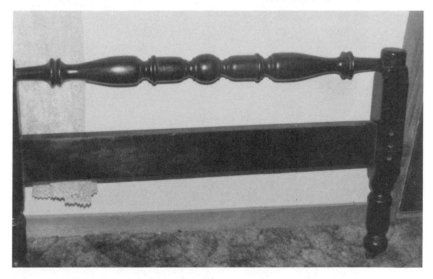

DOUBLE BED
Poplar, walnut stained; complete with side rails; applied moldings at top and base; both posts are attached to side rails; applied decorations. Headboard — 84"h x 59"w. Baseboard — 39"h x 59"w. $895.00 up.

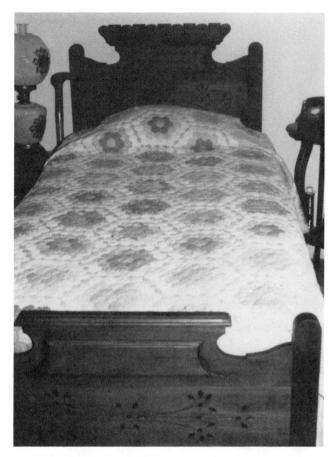

BED
Walnut; Eastlake style; sawtooth cuts and deep flower incisings; found in western Kentucky. Headboard — 45"h x 79"l x 34½"l. Baseboard — 25"h x 79"l x 34½"w. $450.00.

WASHSTAND/ COMMODE
Eastlake style; walnut; pulls have been re-gilded; splashback on the marble top, and above that is a tilting mirror with side "wings" (Gothic type crockets) and a carved and incised pediment and crest; burl inlay; readings; casters on iron. Chest — 18½"w x 13½"dp. $675.00.

COMMODE
Ca. 1860; walnut with applied burl on doors, drawers, and front
post tops; gray and white marble shelf and gallery which has 2
candle shelves; self wood knobs and brass casters. 38"h x 29"w x
19"dp. $600.00.

CHIFFONIER/DRESSER

Mahogany and birdseye maple; drawers all have maple bottoms; piece was refinished and unsightly veneer removed from one drawer — (the short deep one second down on the right) — revealing the plain mahogany base; rare bombé sides; nicely proportioned adjustable mirror is wood pinned to a wishbone frame having brass cornucopias; all fixtures are burnished brass; cabriole legs with feet on wooden casters; applied molding and reverse crest on apron. 50"h x 39"w across shelf x 20"dp. $875.00.

CHIFFONIER
Ca. 1870. Walnut, burl veneered, fully dovetailed drawers; furniture of the finest quality; ornamental brass pulls; unique locking device on the right side hinged post (full height of the piece) that when unlocked, causes the post to be swung back, unlocking each of the seven drawers; then, in reverse, it locks them again and the post appears in its original position; reeding, 2-panel sides; top ledge overhang; posts have matched top and base swells and rings at front. 52"h x 36"w, shelf is 38"w. $1,275.00.

DROPFRONT DRESSER
Ca. 1870; poplar; candle shelves; adjustable mirror; Eastlake style; ebonized and brass collared teardrop drawer pulls have brass escutcheons; the angel-winged pediment has a crest with a designed shield; reedings. 72"h x 40"w x 18"dp. $895.00.

DRESSER
Walnut; burl inlays; "Grand Rapids Renaissance" or factory modified Renaissance; the two drawers on each side of the marble shelf, usually for small articles as gloves, handkerchiefs, fans, etc., have wood knobs, while the long drawers have teardrop pulls of brass; all escutcheons are of wood; incisings on drawer-center panels; with no evidence of an original attached mirror, the bureau was undoubtedly supplied with one hung right above on the wall. 37½"h x 38"w x 18"dp. $450.00.

DRESSER/BUREAU

Cheval glass style (long, narrow, tilting mirror that was sometimes removed from the bureau and hung separately); solid cherry; dovetails, incisings, reeded posts, factory carved applied trims, and brass hardware. Drawer escutcheons evidenced locked drawers (keys lost). Shown by mail order houses as single units or as part of bedroom groups; casters were offered free of charge if the buyer desired them. 70"h x 48"w x 22½"dp. $600.00.

DRESSER
Eastlake style; ca. 1890; plain and flame mahogany veneers; brown and white veined marble; paneled sides; all dovetailed at four-corners drawers are bottom-lined birdseye maple; new brass escutcheons and drawer pulls; reeded posts; applied carvings and deep incisings, heart scallops; sausage rolls and deep finger grooving. Found in York, Pennsylvania; large gallery cornice — cornices said to indicate quality in furniture. 75"h x 33"w x 19"dp. $795.00.

DRESSER
Burl inlays in walnut; Renaissance substyle; self wood knobs differ to size of the drawers which are all lined in pine; carved and incised elaborate crest with broken pediment having a butterfly center; tilting mirror held with wood pins; candle shelves; china casters. 72"h x 40½"w. $675.00.

DRESSER

Pine; unusual to find such pieces made of this wood; fretwork crest (most made with a jigsaw) on adjustable mirror held with wooden pins; acorn below heavily fluted crest; lifttop boxes on shelf held gloves and other small grooming accessories; keys gone which originally could lock four drawers; carved wood "mustache" drawer pulls; roundels, and bracket feet. 72"h x 37½"w 18"dp. $395.00.

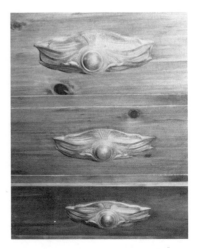

VANITY/DRESSING TABLE

Oak; glass knobs and brass escutcheons on two swell-front veneered drawers; tilting oval mirror held by reverse-S uprights; new white china casters; quarter cut wood; note shaped front legs and straight back legs. 54"h x 36"w x 20"dp. $675.00.

LADIES' CLOTHES BRUSH (Center)

Flower embossings on a silver back with long soft bristles; engraved initials are: "J.L.T." 1½"h x 1¾"w x 7"l. Shop priced at $15.00.

LADIES' CLOTHING BRUSH (Bottom)

At a larger shop in a city was another of the brushes, this more utilitarian-looking with its wooden back and shorter, although equally soft, bristles. Embossed with letters in a lighter stain on the basic black stained wood we can plainly read: "Mack's Ladies Ready-to-Wear, 126 Falls St., Niagara Falls, N.Y. ... You Pay Less Here ... Coats, Suits, Dresses, Waists"; brushes like these kept felt hats groomed and were used to smooth the delicate trimmings. 1¾"h x 7¾"l. $32.00.

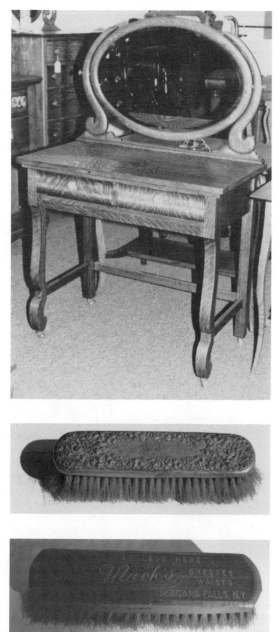

DRESSING TABLE/VANITY

Ca. 1880's; walnut; 4-corner dovetailed drawers
have walnut bottoms; the beauty of the piece is
an adjustable arched Cottage mirror with
reeded uprights and tall finials; double-spool
turned shafts with Duncan Phyfe splayed legs.
(Duncan Phyfe, a prominent cabinetmaker in
New York until about the early 1850's experi-
enced the fading in popularity of the late Classical styles — and the emergence of inevitable
factory takeovers of independent cabinetmakers). 62½"h x 40"w x 18"dp. $795.00.

A drawer may have held such a box of various sized hairpins in thin wire rip-
pled to hold and remain in the long hair fashionable in Victoriana. Here a
portion is still left of the original paper covering with faded indecipherable
maker's lettering. Found in a western New York state Red Barn Antiques
Shop, where it was a joy not knowing which aisle to browse first! Tagged @
$7.50 complete.

GENTLEMAN'S GROOMING MIRROR
Maple and tiger maple; acorn knobbed wooden pins hold the adjustable mirror; egg-and-dart centers decorate the stubby feet; the handsomely designed uprights are uncommon; scalloped base; usually set on top of a chest or flat-top bureau. 20"h x 18"w. $275.00.

SHOE BRUSH
To conclude the chap's grooming before leaving his bedroom, this brush is kept handy for a quick swipe across his shoes. Such brushes were often given away as premiums when clothing or shoes were purchased. 8½" x 2½"w; stiff animal bristles. $38.00.

HIP BATH

Ca. 1890's; dark enameled iron with a white lining and rounded edges. 20"h x 30"l x 29"w. $250.00. A full size bath tub could generally only be found in a home of those having substantial means (or a Bath Parlor attached to a Tonsorial/Barber Shop as we see in old time western movies), it ordinarily would've been set in a bedroom on at least a second floor, requiring lots of containers of both steaming hot and cooler water to be toted (usually by the "hired girl") up lots of stairs to fill it. In families of lesser means (or by preference if a coal burner kept the room warmer) a tin or galvanized washtub put down in the kitchen would've sufficed and emptying out the sudsy water after one (or more) family members had bathed certainly was no cinch either!

ARMOIRE

A very elegant piece in walnut; gilt over the wood; much of the diversified characteristics of the Renaissance Revival; inside shelves; two doors each with unusually wide glass mirrors with extra-wide beveling edges; note the applied corner carvings and reeded and fluted groovings on each of the doors; the rare center front foot matches the crest; several shells; ornamentations; brief cabriole side front legs ending in knurl feet. 96"h x 48"w. $2,995.00 up.

46

GERMAN "SHRANK" (WARDROBE)

Repainted in the style of T. F. Rossler during the early 1800's; shade variations of old blues, deep greens in the leaves, blacks, whites, red, browns, and mustard yellows; black iron hardware with one very large key for each of the escutcheons on the two narrow doors; these latter have various applied decorations with the bust of a woman on one and the bust of a man on the other, each bead-framed; four inside shelves; random width back boards; generous cornice with center applied carvings; straight front, 6"w rounded embellished corners. A rarity. Seen in a Florida shop. 74"h x 57"w straight front x 20"dp. $4,000.00.

ARMOIRE

Veneered walnut in the Gothic Revival style of the French with solid brass ormolu, fluting and reeding; top corner finials balance the sunburst crest; mirror; inside are wood ledges for five shelves; brass pulls on the two side doors. 82"h x 54"w x 16½"dp. $1,150.00.

SINGLE DOOR WARDROBE

English waxed pine. Dealer's comment: "Would make a great pantry!" Reflects a Colonial Revival influence; double tier reeded cornice; brass fixtures; oval applied self wood, the simple decoration adding dignity; an oval mirror at center door; black iron pull the only elaborate feature; 3 inside shelves. 72"h x 21"w x 13½"dp, 13"w boards full height form each side. $695.00.

WARDROBE

Ca. 1840; handfashioned in heart-pine; sometimes these called clothespresses; tongue and groove construction; one shelf and clothes bar inside; has the original key, which works; the set-in mirror may have been added later. 74"h x 40"w x 22½"dp. $995.00.

WARDROBE

Pine; traces of former white paint in wood's tenacious pores; Eastlake style; incisings, and fancy large brass drawer knobs; one of the two missing teardrop door pulls was found so it is shown lying on the corner of an open reeded drawer — repro hardware is being made so the other can be replaced — the mirrored side accommodates floor length garments — the other door opens to reveal shelves; new white china casters; one side doortop will be repaired. 84"h x 43"w x 17½"dp. $650.00 as is. More when entirely restored, depending on repair costs.

LINEN PRESS, also called and used as an ARMOIRE
French influence; walnut; rare mirrored double doors framed in curved wood; burl inlays; note insides of the two doors; and front of the low pullout drawer which could be locked — two original keys are available for that and the doors — lighter wood on the sides in a geometric pattern; fluted top with a lavish pediment and projecting cusp-like corner ornaments; front cabriole legs carrying heavily carved leaf-like patterns applied, and resting on double-scrolled feet on pads. 98"h x 50"w x 18"dp. $3,200.00.

CABINET
Handcarved mahogany with brass drawer pulls and a light brown mottled marble top; Renaissance Revival style; wood casters; could also be called a "chest." 31"h x 21½"w x 14"dp. $850.00.

CABINET
An inlaid medallion, half on each of two drawers; drawers have dovetailed corners and gilt handles; gilt also in the apron decoration as well as on the stiles; swell front; delicate Chippendale style legs; light wood; curved cream marble top with darker grain. 30"h x 26¼"w x 14"dp. $795.00.

TOBACCO CABINET

Ca. 1850; Germanic flavoring in this example of the French Renaissance Revival that spread all over Europe; beginning with a chalcedony top, the rest of the medieval-tinged design for the cased piece combines copper, bronze, and iron with gold velvet lining the bronze-knobbed doors under bronze ornamentation; the pierced low gallery's small crest corresponds with an inverted one at the center of the apron; each side door has the figure of a goddess wearing a fantastic headdress, her hair center parted, and long tresses flowing below her waist; her outstretched arms hold large cups aloft; cloaked in flower strewn draperies, her body rests on a column that in turn rests on the capped head of a vassal (note there is a slight difference in the slope of the cap's edge rolls); there are classic columns with dentils, rampant lions, wreaths and garlands, bowknots, and heraldic family shield patterns; the center knight in full armor has his face guard lowered, revealing expressive facial features (as are those of the ladies); the knight rests the point of his heavy broadsword on the ground; his important rank is further delineated by Prince of Wales feathers; seemingly delicate legs of the cabinet extending from the shelf to the deer feet bases are of iron with three supporting lengths, providing unexpected rigidity, the two legs at the rear are a bit more splayed than those at front, scarcely discernible. (Must have given the maker of this furniture beauty a lot of well deserved satisfaction to complete it.) 46"h x 25"w x 12"dp. $1,375.00.

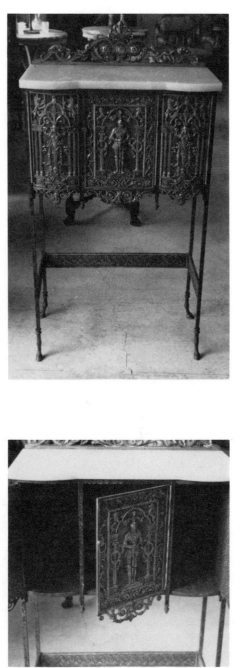

FORMAL CABINET

Victorian Buhl Work, the name referring to an eighteenth century cabinetmaker, André Charles Boulle (also spelled Buhl), who decorated his furniture with inlays of wood on other woods, ivory, shells, yellow and white metals, and tortoise shell, in many designs including scrolls, rope moldings, and acanthus leaf patterns. Here we also find lavish ormolu, broken columns in angled sides, and at the center of the lower doors is a ballet figurine in gold; very large flat button ebonized front feet and at the back they are bracket type; basically the cabinet is ebonized wood; acanthus crest. 84"h x 42"w x 15½"dp. $3,900.00.

DISPLAY CASE — CABINET

Louis XV Revival in graceful white and gilt covered wood with a flat front and swell-sides of glass, the lower portions of the three all handpainted in brightly colored French scenics — a courting couple at center seated on a bench; lavish crest on the pediment with a heavily fluted cornice overhang and a small inverted crest at the center of the apron; all four of the cabriole legs have ormolu trims. 73½"h x 28"w x 17"dp. $1,295.00.

CHINA CABINET

Walnut with burl veneers; beading trim; convex glass sides and flat front; four shelves — top also provides a useful display surface; has the original key. 60"h x 41"w, each of the sides is 16"dp. $975.00.

CURIO/WHATNOT CABINET

Mahogany; brass pull; applied leaf spray crest atop the wide beveled mirror whose oval frame rests on an incised cutout middle shelf pediment; Y-curves hold candle shelves; worn green velvet is on the lower inside glass door shelf; graceful cabriole legs extend from the upper shelf, set in to support the lower oval and thence on to the floor. 53"h x 22"w x 8⅞"dp. $635.00.

CURIO CABINET
Oak with self knobs and brass hardware; applied factory carvings on plain and quarter-cut wood; swell-front glass sides with wood shelves; front animal legs and paw feet; back curved, all with new white china casters. 40"h x 44"w x 16"dp. $795.00.

HANGING WALL CABINET
Grooved cornice provides a wide top shelf for this walnut piece; 1800's typical ornate brass drawer pulls; wood door knob hiding inside shelves; fluted and reeded. 45½"h x 25¾"w x 10"dp. $395.00.

CLOSED CUPBOARD

Ca. 1850's; walnut dyed poplar; imitates ventilation afforded by pie safes; this has four fine-screened 2½"dia holes on each side of the two panelled cupboard sides; a black iron sliding latch controls the position of the two convex curved glass doors (unusual) while brass knobs suffice on the bottom doors; four corner dovetailed drawers wear fancy handles and a simple applied "fountain" graces the top under a wide grooved cornice; larger items can be stored back of the doors on two shelves; side posts continue to form the feet. 72"h x 40"w x 17"dp. $825.00.

CUPBOARD/CABINET
Poplar; exposed black iron door hinges and wood knob pulls; ca. mid-1800's; for ventilation for foods stored herein, two fine-screened large holes on each 1-board-length side; five shelves behind glass doors; bracket feet; 1-board top. 72"h x 38¾"w x 16"dp; 5½"dia holes. $685.00.

STEPBACK CUPBOARD
Ca. 1850–60; walnut; convenient work shelf; concealed hinges and brass knobs; three shelves inside each door section; set-in curved apron; the arch-curves lend attractiveness to a simple cabinet. 66½"h; shelf — 38½"w; top — 11"dp; base — 19½"dp. $595.00.

CONSOLE CHEST/TABLE

Made in the 1840's fashionable style of Louis XV Revival; ebonized mahogany heavily ormolu decorated; two lower deep dovetailed drawers with dull finish brass button pulls extend clear across the front of the chest to include burl inlays, dots-and-dashes, profuse foliage patterns along with wreaths and other such applied embellishments — all combining to make a startling lovely chest; a set-on top of coral and white veined marble is the perfect complement for this object; solid heavy brass feet — even at the back. Particularly note the placement of the base center arrangement almost touching the floor. 40"h x 59½"w. $4,200.00.

CHEST OF DRAWERS
Ca. 1840's; Empire Revival influenced; flat and swell-fronts with handsomely matched crotch (flame) veneering; large wood pulls on grooved backings; two sides egg and two sides angled spool turnings frame a center drop-cover security unit that could be locked with a key in the brass escutcheon; valanced skirt; projecting flat-front base drawer; all drawer corners are dovetailed. 44½"h x 45"w at shelf x 20"dp. $895.00.

GENTLEMAN'S CHEST
Ca. 1860's; hand detailed cherry; carvings applied of flowers, fruit, and leaves; ten ring-grooved brass knobs on dovetailed drawers; Empire Revival influence; 14"dia ball turnings on all four feet with 12"dia cups; chamfer-edged overhang top is a single board 20"w. 63"h x 45"w x 20"dp. $975.00.

CHEST OF DRAWERS

Mahogany with various veneering grains; two flat-front drawers and the others bowfront, including the stiles; the dealer will replace the four missing self-wood knobs on dovetailed drawers; there are holes where an adjustable mirror or low narrow-width gallery was probably attached, but no evidence either has been there for a long time; this Empire Revival influenced chest dates ca. 1870–80; front paw feet with plain feet at the back; white china casters are new. Empire has its own considerable space in cultural progression, peaking about the mid-1800's. 46"h x 38½"w x 20"dp. $595.00.

CHEST OF DRAWERS
Ca. 1840; Empire Revival influenced; simplicity of design suggests a country maker; three long and two shorter dovetailed drawers; the knobs are all self wood — one on a long drawer is half split off; each compartment could have been locked but now the keys and the keepers are missing; thick whorl legs; at one lower side a brass pull opened a "hidden" security space; mahogany. 46"h plus the 7½"h gallery; 45½"w; 20"dp. $725.00.

CHEST OF DRAWERS — or BLANKET CHEST, however used. Ca. mid-1800's, Empire Revival influenced; cherry; self-wood knobs; paneled sides and spool turnings on the projecting corner uprights; generous storage accomodation; mortised corners on the top drawer, dovetails on those below; large ball feet. 38"h x 39½"w x 16½"dp. $435.00.

CHEST OF DRAWERS
Walnut with burl veneers; Empire Revival style; plain and grooved bowfront drawers; wood knobs; beaded molding frames the 7"h x 8"w droplid door which has a lock but key gone; projecting button-turned tops of posts. (Dealer just set a mirror there). 40"h x 41½"w x 19½"dp. $425.00.

CHEST OF DRAWERS
Eastlake style; poplar stained black; incised floral sprays, reeded posts, standout base. 31½"h x 38"w x 18½"dp. $165.00.

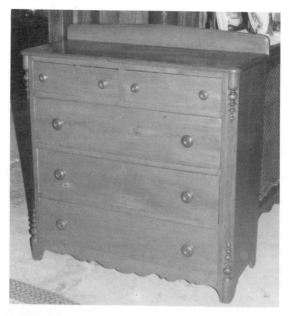

CHEST OF DRAWERS
Maple and cherry; ca. mid-1800's; a simple design with plain low gallery; two-sized self wood knobs; drawers dovetailed in all four corners, scalloped apron, and applied turnings; sides are each one piece wood. 34"h x 32"w x 15"dp.

CHEST of DRAWERS or BLANKET CHEST
Ca. 3rd quarter Victoriana; popular "mustache" pull, here in leaves and nuts for dovetailed drawers; valanced skirt extending to bracket feet; low gallery at back of shelf. 41"h x 40"w x 18"dp. $675.00.

DOWRY/BLANKET/HOPE CHEST

This Empire Revival influenced cedar lined walnut piece with its lighter wood inlaid veneered shield, applied brass floral sprays, egg and dart border, lockable lifttop with a key now missing, and its handsome base variations — was called a Depression Chest, due to its originating during the severely depressed economic times of the 1930's. 21"h x 47"w x 21"dp. $345.00.

Such dowry chests have progressed through the centuries from small boxes and baskets into modern furniture objects. First owned wherever they could be afforded, whether factory made, home made or inherited, they were filled with linens, bedding, and pretty needlework efforts by girls waiting for marriage and a home of their own to run. Victorians were devoted to covering every possible furniture surface with antimacassars to protect sofas and chairs from men's hair oil, crocheted fancies as tablecloths for "show," usually, and tidies and doilies of tatting and knitting. Among the Pennsylvania Dutch, the Dower Chests were customarily made by the prospective bridegroom, who placed on them the family insignia the couple planned to paint on barns and/or other outbuildings, known today as "Hex Marks."

DESK/TABLE

For parlor or home library; plain and quarter sawn oak; a rarity in the popular Victorian "Japanese Infatuation" (or fad) ca. 1876–1900; chamfered edges on the surface with a pierced valance; on the brass drawer pull's escutcheon is the incised head of an Oriental warrior; spool turnings comprise the columns on two underside shelves; applied carvings; tiny spool spindles between reeded center stretcher lengths and at each side stretcher; bun feet on white china casters. 32"h x 40½"w x 26"dp. $795.00.

LADIES' WRITING DESK

Walnut in French Revival influences with burl inlays and gilded brass ornamentation, the framing of the inlay panels resembling the bark of trees; the cabinetmaker's meticulous attention to detail is clearly apparent; hinged dropfront panel becomes a writing surface and could have been locked had the key survived; four cabriole legs wider at top diminish into narrower dimensions at base with tiny toed feet — and only those at front have heavy trim at the top, it, too, extending and narrowing to the base — the ormolu following the size of the legs (you may enjoy surmising what the form of the ornamentation is meant to be — to me the top, at least, resembles a lizard's or dragon's head); a low gallery was put on in section and connected. 36"h x 18"w x 16"dp. $850.00 up.

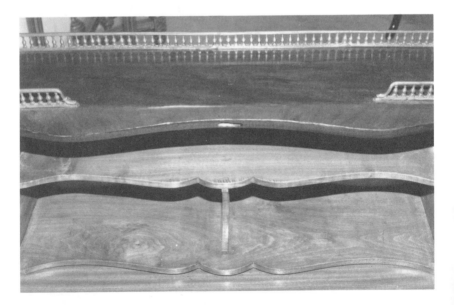

S-ROLL TOP DESK

A big plus is its having the original brass key, locking the (often known as) "curtain" (for "Curtain Roll Desk") — the wood strips placed horizontally on a flexible backing which, of finest quality wood, moved easily up and down, covering the writing surface and individual compartments and dovetailed drawers under the lid; sides are paneled, spade-type legs. These are still popular today. 48"h x 54½"w x 32"dp. $1,375.00.

PLANTATION DESK
Ca. 1840; walnut and cherry; forward slanted lift top is
the writing surface, covering a deep well; doors can be
locked with the original key; self wood knobs; probably
made by a southern cabinetmaker — or even someone
"right on the place" trained to do such work. Back then
were also itinerant cabinetmakers, using wood cut and
air-dried on the plantations themselves. 78"h x 41½"w x
30½"dp. $1,445.00.

SECRETARY-DESK
Ca. 1870; follows Eastlake trend to square lines; walnut with burl inlays; deep incisings; architectural leanings in the upright columns and arched pediment with reeded sides and center roundel flower; casters; bric-a-brac ledge above front-covered shallow storage spaces; brass pulls and escutcheons for which there is no longer a key. 59"h x 29"w. $895.00.

SECRETARY-DESK

Mahogany with lighter wood inlays and applied escutcheons; brass knobs and "earring" pulls on mortised drawers as well as pullout side supports for a writing ledge — and to slide the wooden slatted "curtains" sideways, displaying the cubbyholes; four circular drawer handles are white porcelain centers on blue frames, all edged with dull brass. A brass eagle on a globe centers the shaped gallery with matching globe finials at each side. 78"h plus the eagle and globes. $1,295.00.

A Sheraton Revival type. Thomas Sheraton, 1751–1800, was an English author and furniture designer who is thought to have been apprenticed to a cabinetmaker. His manuals secured his place in history. Best remembered are his characteristic reeded legs, vertical lines, inlays, and classical preferences.

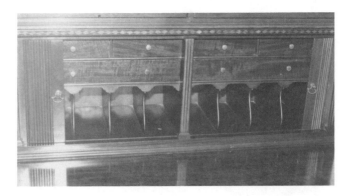

BOOKCASE

Walnut; dull polished brass hardware; rare embellishments; spool turned columns; pierced gallery on third tier; applied carvings and flutings; burl veneered drawer fronts; much detail. Can be locked with the original key. 73"h x 13"dp. $1,995.00.

PARTNERS DESK

Each side of this oak double desk is the same; a 4" wide frame borders a
leather surface with no center seam; these framed edges retard shrinking
and warping; polished solid brass drawer pulls, much used on utilitarian furniture from the late 1800's into the 1900's; one side tall S-roll pulls up to cover
a deep storage unit; it can be locked but since the piece just came to the
dealer's shop, there's been no time to repair the lock — so it's handheld for
the picture; found in Pennsylvania. 31"h x 59"w x 51"dp. $1,285.00.

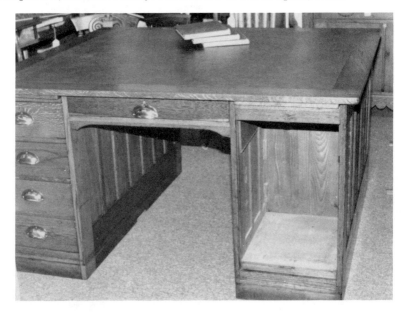

POSTMASTER'S DESK

Made of solid black walnut, its slanted writing surface is separate lift tops that cover storage compartments; doors below are access to larger storage spaces; four legs are ring-turned, bulge-centered posts, similar to those smaller patterns in the gallery spindles. Characteristic in general of country cabinetmakers of the period, still reaching back into Colonial Revival influences, this desk reflects the down-to-earth wholesomeness of rural life.

And for its distinctive place in earlier Victoriana, "as the story goes": In the year 1815 Peter Tower, a cabinetmaker and farmer, settled land in far northwestern New York state. Later he became the local postmaster, conducting postal services in his cabin, where, on its regular journeys along that trail, the stagecoach dropped off the mail. Peter himself built this desk from walnut wood cut on his own place, at what became Towers Corners. Still later, during construction of a larger home, the desk was relegated to an upstairs room. Years went by and as so often happens with heritage pieces the desk was offered at an auction "sold where it stood." Great grandchildren purchased it, and when they went to pick it up, it couldn't be moved out through the door — nor through the window — not until casement and window had both been removed. With the aid of a tractor, the desk left the farm on the bed of a truck — to be refinished and given by the family to the town hall at Towers Corners. 53"h x 38"w. Museum piece, no price. A piece of this origin and excellence, refinished as has been done here, would have a high value.

STANDUP MIRROR
Overall patterned cast iron frame with slightly marred glass whose back adjustable iron bar enabled upright usage, or being laid flat for storage. 11"h x 17"w. $145.00.

An ancient Roman or Greek might use highly polished metal. Glass for mirrors was available in the Middle Ages, large quantities produced in Venice from the 1500's. Their reflective backing was a thin coating of metal (for instance, tin and mercury mixed together); earlier metals were replaced with silver ca. 1840's. Plate glass appearing for very large mirrors during the 1600's influenced such "fixed" pieces to be generally classified as "home furniture."

MIRROR
In the ornate style of typical Victorian Rococo Revival, a rare Rose Medallion surrounded by luscious carvings and applied motifs; heavily gilt wood frame. 67"h x 30½"w. $1,995.00.

From the elegant to the elegantly plain:

THE ELEGANT MIRROR
About 130 yrs. old; Louis XV Revival's lavish style in gilt and some gold leaf on wood; wood backing; fluted molding and intricately designed pediment. 80"h x 46"w. $1,495.00.

AND THE ELEGANTLY PLAIN MIRROR
Deeply grooved walnut frame; glass is gilt framed. 38"h x 32"w. $198.00.

WALL MIRROR

Cast bronze frame in Rococo Revival style with dots, leaves, and swirls; scratches and dampness discolorations on the glass can easily be made to appear in perfect condition. Today a glass repair shop can set a comparable sized piece of new mirror glass behind this old one. In most cases, this will restore the appearance and functioning without destroying or removing the original — and not betraying the new glass behind. 17"h x 11"w. $165.00.

WALL MIRROR

Gilt lined walnut frame; applied cutout crest. The term "mirrors" was not in common usage until the latter 1800's, always before that they were called "looking glasses." 38"h x 32"w. $210.00

WALL MIRROR
Shadow box style; walnut and gilt with incised burl inlays; near-mint glass; 3¼" deeply reeded frame; backing is one piece of thin wood. 29½"h x 23¼"w. $215.00.

MIRROR
Walnut frame with applied factory rosettes at each corner; thought to have originally been a bureau mirror as there is a 1⅜" inset brass pin left near a 1-side top as were these fasteners for tilting mirrors on large cased pieces. 32¾"h x 22½"w. $75.00.

HAT RACK
Brass; four individual light coat holders with button ends kept clothing from slipping off; these partial-S-curves continue up to form hat stands above. (Heavy garments might tip over the rack.) These have remained popular furniture objects, in demand today. 59½"h. $95.00. Many being reproduced.

TOWEL RACK
Ca. 1890; walnut; hand-beaded panel, gilt bordered. Eastlake style. 19"w x 4½"dp. $225.00.

SHELF
Walnut with black stained contrasts; applied carved molding and antlered buck's head; incised leaves and swirls with heart centers; found near Lake Ontario. 20"h x 18"w x 7½"dp shelf. $110.00.

BOOK RACK
Walnut; rare to find these pieces with such extensive embellishments — applied gilt carvings, handles are also book restraints at ends; large end roundel and smaller gilt rosette; S-curves, floral and leaf designs plus toed lion feet; rope edged top shelf 13"w and deep book/magazine well. 27½"h x overall 24½"w. $210.00.

BEDDING (QUILT) RACK
Ca. 1800; walnut with uncommon side crests; silk and velvet "Crazy Quilt" for display; a sturdy rack. 38"h x 26½"w x 10"dp. $85.00.

BEDDING (QUILT) RACK
Walnut; simply designed with ball and button turnings. Bedding not needed for bed at night would be hung over the racks — or those treasured pieces only put on beds during daytime for "show." 36"h x 9"w at top. $85.00.

CABINET ORGAN
Walnut; applied carvings; fretwork music holder; when no longer needed as a
musical instrument, a large storage compartment was built into the open
space intended for pedal operation. And there is more: many, many years ago
a small church was one of the first established when Lewiston in northwestern New York state was growing from an important fur trading post on the
Niagara Frontier near Lake Ontario into a settlement then into a thriving
town. There, later in its own tenure, this little organ faithfully and tunefully
enhanced the gatherings of an expanding population. And then, as tales of
heritage poignantly recall, of one of the weddings there it is said: "The bride,
a personal maid of Jenny Lind, wore as her gloves at the ceremony a beautiful gift pair from the Swedish Nightingale." Finally, as more space was
imperative, the small church was closed. Today its doors have opened, but to
receive guests as a museum wherein the little organ again occupies an hon-
ored place, though mute now — the haunting echoes of its melodies heard
only with the heart. No Price. Museum quality.

PUMP (CABINET) ORGAN

Eastlake style; walnut; velvet covers in iron push pedals and back of the fretwork above and below keyboard; many rosettes, turnings, reeding, finials, and inlays. A wide gallery crest has pointed and squared edging cutouts and a center of half a sunburst and small finial. An 11½"w bar at each side makes for more convenient lifting and moving the organ. In the Middle Ages organ building was centered in the Byzantine Empire; the nineteenth century saw crescendo and "swell" pedals commonly employed in the construction of organs. 67¼"h x 44½"w. $795.00.

ORGAN

Found in Maine; walnut cabinet style; worn-through plush on iron pump pedals; many turnings; high center mirror. 80"h x 44½"w x 23½"dp. $595.00.

PIANO (PIANOFORTE, piano meaning soft, forte meaning strong)
Rosewood; top front panel and fretwork music stand fold down flat to cover
keys when piano not in use; lyre with pedals in wood and iron; ivory keys are
all in mint condition; thickly hipped cabriole legs have applied moldings and
shields with double scrolled feet above inverted lined cup bases. 32"h x 45"w
x 2½"dp. $1,050.00.
The first piano was made ca. 1709, a Florentine upright early in the nineteenth century, and the mechanical upright piano developed early in the
1800's. In Late Victoriana and early twentieth century this last was sur-
passed by the phonograph and radios.

UPRIGHT PIANO
Mahogany with brass pedals; full keyboard — also has the added feature of a player piano — (200 rolls included); by the early 1890's this country had produced and shipped here and overseas pianos and organs of all types numbering many thousands. 54"h x 58½"w x 26"dp. $1,450.00.

PIANO or ORGAN FLOOR LAMP
These were almost standard purchases with the musical instruments — useful as well as very decorative; it has several Patent Dates in the latter 1800's, days and months too age-dimmed to be read; of elaborately cast brass with a red glass globe, it originally burned kerosene — now electrified. $350.00.

MUSIC CABINET

Mahogany with brass fixtures; has the original key and keeper; gallery has applied ribbon garlands and a center bellflower with bowknot crest and fretwork ribbons; top shelf has finial posts while those at center shelf resemble a tall fluted child's spinning top; the mirror has an unusually wide bevel; a chain-held drop front with applied leaf scrolls and beading decor covers a shelf and an extra ledge for another; open lower shelves have turned posts that stand out slightly and have dog feet carvings. 57"h x 21" w x 14"dp. $595.00.

SEWING MACHINE
Oak and newly repainted to the original blackened iron; on lattice pedal: "New Royal"; serpentine curved top and bow front drawers each side; brass knobs and applied trim. 30"h x 33"w closed. 17½" dp. $285.00.

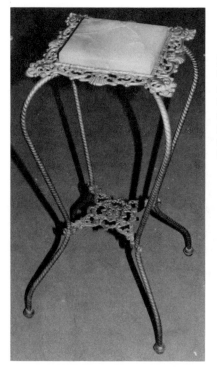

FERN STAND
Gilt cast iron; wide lacy shelf frames a
shaded white and darker marble
square, all in a Rococo substyle; roped
serpentine legs with sleighbell feet fasten a small star-shaped shelf. Marble
square 8". 30"h x top 13"sq x shelf 7"sq.
$325.00.

FERN or LAMP STAND
Green marble top, lower shelf, and
Corinthian columned uprights; cast
iron gilded fixtures while the legs S-
curve to Louis XV style feet. Shelves
— 31"h x 14"sq. $495.00.

FERN STAND
Mahogany base, veneered top; heavily turned and reeded shaft with three scroll top Duncan Phyfe type reeded legs; also popular Bible stands. $165.00.

PEDESTAL
Walnut; turned post and cutout squared base with casters. 36"h x 13" dia top. $215.00.

FERN STAND
Walnut; reeding and turnings; the heavy legs are needed to hold big pots of greenery — or whatever the homemaker wishes. 42½"h x 12" dia top. $145.00.

PEDESTAL
Walnut with larger than usual spool turning on the post; also has flat button feet under the 3-tiered base; chamfered edge top. 34"h x 8½"sq top. $145.00.

PLANT STAND (or for Bible or other book)
Ca. 1875; after the 1876 Philadelphia Centennial Victorians became intensely enamored of the Japanese craze, and there was not enough reed and bamboo, so makers turned maple and oak wood, grooving and staining it to look like bamboo; edging is not original — the painted top is. 30"h x 16" dia top. $145.00.

FERN STAND
Ca. 1840; Empire Revival influenced; white and deep gray marble with an octagonal base and only rings to enhance the plain stone. Seen in north-central Georgia; a popular furniture object in homes able to afford them. 40½"h x 10" dia. $495.00.

PEDESTAL
Solid onyx with gilt; borrowing from a Renaissance style of the ancient formal column forms, such as Corinthian, Doric, and Ionic. 30"h x 15" sq top and base. $1,700.00.

STATUE
Bronze recast lady who stands atop this column is No. 11 of a limited edition, modern made, typical of Victorian elegant decor; she is standing on an earth platform, wind seemingly blowing her skirts, holding a basket of cherries in each hand. 54"h. $5,700.00.

BRONZE GODDESS of JUSTICE

By Mayer. Gilded metal with black tin pan scales and thin iron chains; green marble base; standing on a serpent coiled in a grassy mound over grooved layers of earth. 23"h (The signature of Mayer is a plus). $1,700.00.

BUST

Marble in great detail; a winged lion with upcurled tail has one paw held up on a block of marble below the bust — both on a step-cut squared base. The face is beautiful — she has two tiny no-harm cracks. Found in Massachusetts. Statuary as shown in this book was immensely popular with Victorians. Today still being sought, it has long been copied with as many of the original characteristics as possible. 24"h. $1,000.00.

STAND

Cast bronze and gold leaf with porcelain; from ca. 1753 into the Transitional Period of the 1800's, this beauty of the French persuasion typifies the extravagant Rococo Revival. Cast with brightly colored florals, garlands, featherlike curves, and much more, the round post concludes with a three-pronged base having tiny rollers under perfectly cast feet; its top support with a wide collar holds a patterned rim with a recessed groove in which the detailed handpainted Sevres porcelain tray rests; signed: "Gueron"; a flower pattern borders the scene in which a servant steadies a skiff while a courtier assists a fashionable lady into the boat. 29"h x 30" top dia. $2,850.00.

LAMP STAND

Walnut; gray veined white marble top fits on a carved depressed ledge of the grooved rim; straight and thickly turned post on small ball feet. 32½"h overall x 19½" top dia. 17" marble top dia x 18" base dia. $275.00.

CANDLESTAND
Pine in Renaissance Revival style; stamped: "Patented in Canada 1875"; inverted acorn finial at base of center grooved post into which are mortised four legs with knob decorations. 29½"h x 15" top dia. $135.00.

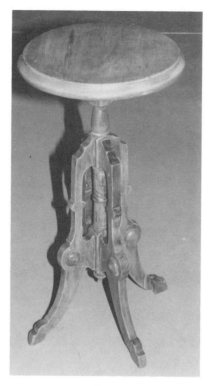

CANDLESTAND
Marble circle fits down onto a groove in the wood rim; walnut with extensive incisings. Eastlake lines. 28"h x 14" top dia. $150.00.

Three CANDLEHOLDERS (sometimes called CANDLESTICKS) that might have stood on such candlestands. Candlesticks were first handfashioned from metals with a point upon which to impale the candle — known as prickets. These were followed by elaborate Rococo types — a socket in which to fit the candle, above a small collar, a wider saucer at base to catch the dripping wax — followed by more staid and plainer columns with heavily weighted bases in the late Victorian era when lamps became more commonplace.

A. CANDLEHOLDER
Silver-washed metal, handmade, with deep saucer, rounded stand, and profusely decorated with small silver bells, it has a dragon's head at the end of each scrolled "wing" holding in its mouth a dangling bell. 5½"h x 2¾" base dia. $135.00.

B. CANDLEHOLDER
Gilt on brass with onyx; fingerhold; tiny splayed feet; feather-like collar and decorated edges of the saucer; Rococo styling, the candle socket resembles flower petals. 8"h x 4" sq base. $195.00.

C. CANDLEHOLDER
Bronze with alabaster; can be unscrewed into three parts; heavy; the whole more dignified column is unobtrusively decorated with turnings, groovings, and carving-like patterns. 12"h x 5"rd base. $225.00.

OCCASIONAL STAND
Walnut with burl inlays, these first factory made during the last of the 1800's — went on into the 1930's — where the legs and feet styles were called "Depression" feet. Grooving — brass knobs. 29½"h x 18" sq. $195.00.

OCCASIONAL STAND
Walnut; one drawer dovetailed in all four corners has a band of circle and dart factory applied carvings; brass ring pull on a rope edged escutcheon; lower shelf; turned legs with flat button rings for decor; chamfered top edges. 30½"h x 13½"sq top. $125.00.

PARLOR TABLE/STAND
Sometimes called a Bible stand;
pale brown and white veined
marble; angled reeded legs on
white china casters; ball turnings at center base joinings;
finial. 30"h x 18¼"w top x
13½"dp. $225.00.

What might have been on a
similar stand:
FAMILY PHOTO ALBUM.
Ca. before 1861; seen in the
parlor of Georgia plantation
home; green velvet over a
heavy paper base center
stamped in a colorful country
scenic; silver catch and clo-
sure. 10"h x 8"w. $145.00.

PICTURE STAND or EASEL
Painted black cast iron in a
horseshoe framed leaf center
pattern on a twig and branches
base. $120.00.

SHAVING STAND
Black painted metal; grooved tilting mirror;
13"dia open circle for setting a basin of
water, with at each side a small arched bar
for a towel, etc.; a pullout drawer on the
center round beneath four depressed circles in which to set shaving accessories; at
the base is a small round "stand" which
could be for a kettle or pitcher; the whole
frame is curved. $650.00.

BIRD CAGE and STAND

Ornate mahogany stand with gilt features; it has a turned post on a fluted 3-way base; unusual to find such an elaborate wooden stand; ball and flat button turnings with three smaller stand finials and a larger one atop the cage; a high fluted arch accommodates the cage's crest. 72"h cage x 16" around. $1,100.00.

PRIE DIEU/PRAYING STAND

Ca. 1890; clear and knotty pine; it's a rest for the elbows, a shelf for a book, purse, etc.; and a bench for the knees; original watered silk pad. 33"h x 18"w slanted top x 6½"dp bench 7½"dp. $128.00 – $188.00 to regions.

FOYER STAND

Dark traces on white marble; a heavy piece; mid to last quarter of Victorian era; stood in the foyer of a Georgia home of substantial means, its main purpose to hold a card receiver (it could also have held a lamp or a statuette.) 30"h top x 16" square — thicker base is 15" square. $1,700.00.

CARD TRAY (CARD RECEIVER)

Ca. 1800's; shortly after the Civil War these were introduced in America for more formal homes, the tray customarily in the foyer sitting on a table or stand as shown herein, to receive calling cards from visitors. In so many areas Victorian "niceties" of behavior were stringent and this was one of them. The tray is gold washed bronze with Cupid and Venus applied on a white onyx plate that was held in a groove with a small depression so the cards would not fall out; lavish French influenced Louis XV embossed; fretwork scrolled projections. 9"h x 16" dia. $1,500.00.

SETTEE
Walnut; original horsehair padding; newly re-upholstered in a Victorian pattern copied from the original with gimp edging; Eastlake factory styling in applied trims, among them incisings, a large round crest with a centered roundel on a winged pediment; wooden casters. 36½"h x 52"w x 22"dp. $750.00.

COUCH
Ca. 1840–60; Empire transitional. Original white silk damask still only slightly soiled; walnut frame; beading, scrolls, applied factory crest open rose and leaves carving; partial tufting. 36"h x 54"w. $1,600.00.

TRIPLE CHAIRBACK SETTEE
Mahogany; in Chippendale Colonial Revival style; pierced splats; the acanthus leaf knee applied carvings enhance four front cabriole legs which terminate in flattened claw and ball feet while only three legs at back have a simple curve ending in spade-like tiny feet. Note there are no stretchers to support this uncommonly long settee; reupholstered in white lightly-patterned fabric. (Chippendale is said to have favored the Gothic styles). 40"h x 60"l x 21"dp x 18"fl. $795.00.

SETTEE
Eastlake style; black walnut with mustard gold velvet upholstery gimp bound and tufted back; tapered legs; iron casters front feet only. (Charles Eastlake favored the Empire Revival lines, but his strenuous efforts at simplifying many of the more excessively embellished Victorian patterns in furniture, while embraced by American manufacturers, often led to parodies of his ideas). 41"h x 56"w x 23"dp. $495.00.

DAY BED/CHAISE LOUNGE

Ca. 1870; walnut, various incisings and carvings on flat-sawn wood surfaces; moss green velvet; casters; splayed block legs. Even before the end of the Civil War, Grand Rapids, Michigan, was an established important furniture manufacturing center, making not only these pieces of plainer lines but also those more sophisticated with many embellishments — thus "Grand Rapids Renaissance" became nationally recognized. 33½"h x 68"l x 22"dp x 14"fl x end headrest slope 23"dp. $675.00.

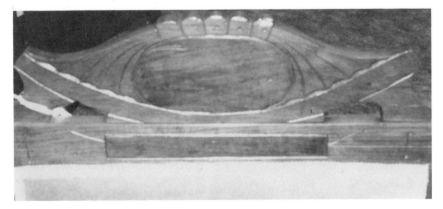

COUCH/DIVAN/LOUNGE
Ca. 1881; walnut; turnings, incisings, button spindles, reeding, floral among the natural and applied carvings; Eastlake styling; well-worn velvet in stripes of green, maroon, and mustard yellow, trimmed with gimp; the one end backrest arm lowers to form a flat couch. 40"h back x 70"l. $695.00.

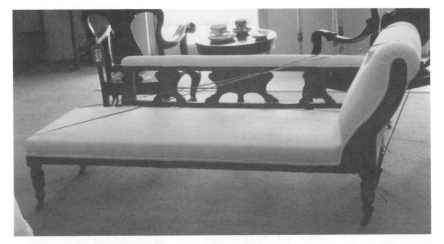

FAINTING COUCH/DAYBED/CHAISE LOUNGE

Found in many Victorian homes at the base of a bed where ladies of tender sensibilities prone to fainting and fatigue could have a nap; reupholstered in pale velvet on a mahogany frame; pierced one-side uprights underarm are uncommon; casters. 31"h x 22"w x 70"l x 14"fl. $595.00.

SOFA

Mahogany; ca. late Empire Revival; in America often referred to as the "Recamier." Mme. Juliette Recamier, a famous French beauty, was painted by Jacques David, as she reclined on a Grecian-roll couch of similar style; the unique arm design was planned to accommodate the cylinder roll bolsters; patterned silk damask has been restored as closely as possible to the original pattern. 30½"h x 73½"l x 9"fl seat apron. $775.00.

MEDALLION BACK SOFA

Tufted red silk patterned upholstery on walnut with a medallion back, as the sofa below; factory produced in innumerable quantities; despite their original quantities available, today the interest in acquiring a piece for private homes and historical museums continues — so still-mint or good sofas don't reside too long in dealers' possessions; New Hampshire found. 42"h x 63"l x 17½"dp. $785.00.

MEDALLION BACK SOFA

Walnut; ca. third quarter of the nineteenth century; oval tufted and plain upholstery in pale silk damask restored to the original; finger rolls and short cabriole legs end in diminished paw feet over casters. During that period, innumerable such pieces were factory produced, many of black walnut frames with horsehair upholstery. (After several years of usage, horsehair was prone to prickle, hairs poking through in spots uncomfortable to encounter, as in my Granny's sofa.) 41½"h x 60"l x 17½"dp x 15"fl. $750.00.

SLEIGH BACK SOFA
Rococo substyle in walnut; factory made during late Victorian era; years ago the rose velvet was replaced to the original; four casters terminating serpentine finger rolls; brief acanthus leaves on headpiece. 36"h x 40"w x 19"dp. $595.00.

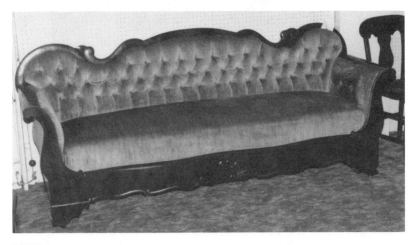

SOFA
Dates about 1840. Transitional Empire into early Victorian in a classical style; mahogany; gold velvet with tufted back; applied molding on bottom of apron with a gracefully curled crest. 34"h x 78"l x 24"dp x 18"fl. $695.00.

SOFA

Victorian influenced by the French Louis XVI Revival; ca. 1840–1880; white and gilt painted mahogany frame with pale blue silk brocade upholstery; tufted back and a plain reversible cushion; leaves on the top and apron; applied blossoms; fluted cabriole legs — footpads at front only; straight back legs of matching length for floor level evenness. 34"h x 53"w x 30"dp. $1,800.00.

SOFA/SETTEE

Renaissance Revival style reflecting those made in midwestern cities such as Grand Rapids 1860–1870 (cities in the east usually produced more elaborate pieces); crimson velvet upholstery with a single tufted row forming back panels — all with gimp edging; applied trims share the decorating with incisings, a shield pediment and a concave carved roundel center that resembles embellishments on classical furniture. 42"h x 51"w x 22"dp. $895.00.

PARLOR SET
Walnut; gold velvet; about the 1890s; pierced underarms;
shield backs; applied factory-type feathery curls with match-
ing pediment on each piece. $750.00 three pc. set.
Settee — 37½"h x 45"w x 20"dp x 9"fl.
Armchair — 37"h x 21½"w front seat x 20"dp x 9"fl.
Side chair — 37½"h x 19"w front x 17½"w back of seat x 11"fl.

PARLOR SET
Three piece set walnut with spring seat construction covered with well-worn pale yellow velvet (gimp needs refastening on front of the chair); Eastlake styling; pierced arm rests; applied carvings on headpiece with roundel at center of back wood divider; iron casters only on front feet. $595.00.

Settee — 38"h x 48"w x 23"dp.
Both chairs — 39"h x 19"w x 20"dp x 18"fl.

PARLOR SET
Ca. 1870; Eastlake influence; walnut; reupholstered; wood casters; applied factory trims including incisings, reeded stiles, turnings, flower roundels terminating arm rests, and pierced splat on settee in the form of crosses; acanthus leaf crests on each headpiece.
Settee — 40"h x 53"w, back section 37"w x 21"dp seat x 18"fl. $648.00.
Side Chair — 37"h x seat 19"w frt x 17"w bk x 18"dp x 17"fl. $298.00.

SOFA

Transitional from our American Federal Period 1800–1815 into this example of Empire Revival 1800–1845; skilled cabinetmakers in these styles active in cities like Annapolis, Pittsburgh, and Baltimore; floral tapestry upholstery; detailed eagle; wide moldings in serpentine lines; groovings on heavy base; typical Empire rolled arms, and huge berry and floral cornucopias. 37"h x 82"l x 17"fl. $1,525.00.

PARLOR SET

Ca. 1875–80; ebonized wood with lovely marquetry designs. While inlays have been attributed to many Revival furniture styles, it was very expensive, but popular with people who could afford to buy "artistic furniture." $975.00.

Settee (newly upholstered) — 33"h x 16"fl

Chair — 33"h x 18"dp x 16"fl

SERVER/BUFFET
Mahogany with a curved white veined marble top and four doors, burnished brass escutcheons; the two center doors both opened with one lock; matched-grain burl veneer and lighter patterned inlays on doors; cabriole legs. (Clear glasses on top could not be removed for picture — ready for a dinner table setting). Louis XVI revival. 39"h x 84"w x 24"dp. $850.00.

SERVER
Ca. 1850; one long four-corner mortised drawer; two smaller drawers four-corner dovetailed; self wood knobs; pine. 39"h x 31"w x 15"dp. $395.00.

SERVER
Mahogany; new white china casters; scalloped apron; wood pulls. 36"h x 36"w x 17½"dp. $295.00.

REPRODUCTION of about 45 yrs. ago. French CONSOLE style to display cleverness of modern cabinetmaker and adherence to the original; mahogany; veined dark and light marble top overhang; inlays and gilded brass ormolu; deep top side drawer and two doors below; opening to spaces for silver, dishes, and other dining accessories — each with a roundel pull. 34"h x 52"w x 21½"dp. $3,995.00.

PIER GLASS TYPE CONSOLE
Overall gilt on wood; lavishly decorated; one-piece solid walnut oval has on it a painted French scenic; marble shelves above three display units with two shelves each — each unit drapery festooned; slim feet reflect the Louis XVI Revival characteristics; seen in Atlanta, Georgia. 10'h x 52"w. $5,900.00.

SIDEBOARD
Ca. 1880; walnut; 56"w dark veined white marble curve front shelf supports an arch framed large mirror above two smaller ones concealing storage spaces; three types of brass hardware; paneled 25"w silver drawers are both four-corner dovetailed. $2,400.00.

SIDEBOARD/CUPBOARD

About 200 years old, used and treasured into the nineteenth century; a rarity; solid walnut; profuse carvings, reedings, incisings, and pierced units covered many motifs — as baskets of fruit, garlands, scrolls, feathers, leafy vines with woody tendrils, acanthus leaves, a drum, pierced crest with an armorial pediment, barley twist stiles, and turnings, etc. — the central theme is the winged lion-headed dragons and the large bats heads (note the cleverly carved expression of the eyes); darker burl inlays top and bottom of each side; finials. Gilded brass escutcheons with missing keys for each of the four doors and the two small drawers; inside shelves below and in the setback section; drawer pulls are the bats' heads; Renaissance Revival styling. 99"h x 55½"w x 21½"dp. $2,395.00.

SIDEBOARD
Solid walnut; Renaissance Revival among the eclectic characteristics; three tiers with stepback shelves; rope and beaded mirror frame; (these large mirrors were made until about 1918–20 when they became generally narrower on buffets and such); here sumptuously carved head to foot cabinetmaker's treasure exudes a Germanic flavor, as New York's Gustav Herter favored in the early Victorian era. Here are innumerable patterns such as urn finials, cornucopias with nuts, fluted scrolls, deep egg and geometric framings, dragons, and those resembling Goddesses; a heraldic center is below the heavy cornice; there are swirls, two narrow tall doors concealing shelves, violins, a pierced apron, and two front feet — each a furred satyr's face — plain at the rear. 98"h x 54"w x 20½"dp. $2,100.00.

STOOL
French influenced with Renaissance Revival type carving on entire mahogany base frame and whorl-feet legs; customarily used on the floor at or near a bed's footboard; Victorians adored these floral patterned silk brocade upholsteries. 17"h x 38"w x 19"dp. $450.00.

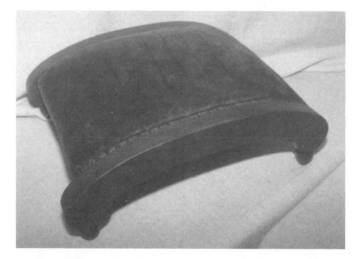

FOOTSTOOL
Dome top curved walnut; somewhat worn in places, the green velvet held by dull brass tacks; ball feet. 4¼"highest point x 13"l curve. $150.00.

PIANO STOOL

Ca. 1870–80; birch and walnut; plain, ball, and button turnings; a heavy piece; fluted seat; three angled uprights support the post on its tapered legs splayed close to the floor, ending in cup and ball feet; revolving seat is adjustable to height. 18½"h at present x 13½"dia seat. $125.00.

PIANO STOOL

Mahogany; angled turned stiles and spindles hold the curved backpiece; flutings; an iron fixture under the seat allows revolving the seat to desired height; the smaller brass feet and claw holding glass ball type are less expensive than larger units. 36"h x 14½"dia seat. $325.00.

ORGAN STOOL
Walnut top frame and post on a 3-legged cast iron cabriole base; reupholstered cushion fits neatly onto the wood frame — patterned as closely as possible to the original eagle motif. 19"h x 14"sq top. $150.00.

ORGAN STOOL
Walnut; revolves; velvet reupholstery. 18"h x seat 16"l x 12"w. $110.00.

ORGAN STOOL
Ca. 1875; walnut; tufted octagonal velvet cushion; seat revolves and adjusts to desired height. 18½"h as is x 14½"top widest dimension. $195.00.

ORGAN STOOL
Walnut; revolves and can be adjusted to various heights; cast iron center post; moss colored velvet covered padded seat with serpentine edges. 20"h x 15"sq top. $185.00.

INVALIDS' STOOL/CHAIR

Walnut; all four sides incised with scrolls each side of a spear head; scalloped base with uprights continuing to form bracket feet; brass fixtures; basic frame is four wide boards; seat grooved to fit chamberpot. 16¾"h x 15½"w x 15¼"dp. $135.00.

INVALIDS'
STOOL/CHAIR

Pine; brass and self wood fixtures; random width boards inside where a chamberpot could be set; coming into early Victoriana from preceding centuries, these stools fashioned often as armchairs with slip seats and wide low aprons to conceal the appliance. With the advent of running water, these stools principally remained for the convenience of invalids. 18"h x 17¼"sq. $145.00.

DINING TABLE
Cherry; from western Kentucky; octagonal pedestal on cutback 4-way base with iron casters (here set on tile floor protectors); chairs not included. 30"h x 42"dia top. $695.00 — value includes two available extension boards.

DUMBWAITER

This is a lift on which serving pieces or food ready for the table could be let up or down by the rope from one story to another or from room to room as seen at the kitchen level of a Victorian home now a museum; when not in use, the 2-panel hinged door was kept closed. No Price.

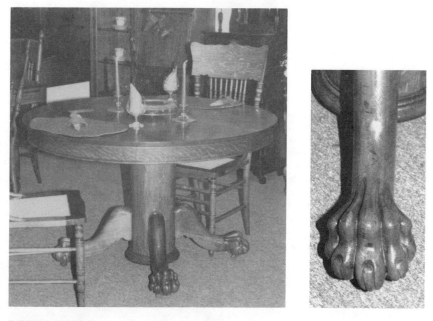

DINING TABLE

Golden oak plain and quarter sawn; thick lions' feet with prominent toes on casters; such tables sought today for country kitchen family meals — and informal entertaining. 30"h x 42"top dia. $775.00 (chairs not included).

TABLE with FOUR CHAIRS
A marriage; here blackened bent iron chairs, which originally probably had thin wood seats, have been more comfortably upholstered in a cotton fabric, these have been called "soda fountain furniture." A new 42"dia wood top has been set on a black-painted iron 30"h New Home sewing machine base. $385.00 set.

ACCENT or OCCASIONAL TABLE
Mahogany; ca. 1850's; dealer described it as a "distinctively rare accent table"; barley twists with shot-ball-size turnings at tops of posts along with rings there and at bases; offset spindles connect the legs to the uniquely edged shelf; note curves of the splayed legs. 29½"h. $425.00.

PARLOR/LAMP TABLE
Mahogany; burl veneered scalloped edge top and carved veneer apron; groovings, and spool turnings; small shelf. 29"h x 19¾"dia top. $395.00.

ACCENT (TEA) TABLE
Walnut; Dutch pad feet; tiny spindles fasten legs to surface; unusual attention paid in designing turned center post in a wooden cup — has inverted base finial. 25¼"h x 14"top dia. $185.00.

TABLE/STAND
Mission style in walnut; squared simplicity; spearhead cutouts; overhang top. (Developed by Gustav Stickley, there were many imitators of his Mission styles.) 28"h x 19"sq. $145.00.

ACCENT TABLE
Cherry; oval in Oriental style popular after the 1876 Philadelphia Exposition; scalloped shallow apron under overhang top; stick and ball spindles on the semi-curved lower shelf. 36"h x 24" widest part of oval. $160.00.

CONSOLE TABLE
Gold washed walnut;
half-turtle top in gray
veined marble; Louis
XV Revival; primarily
floral and leaves;
crosshatch-and-dot
lines; grooved feath-
ery scrolls and a
shield-like pediment
on the apron with a
smaller one in frame
at the joining of the
stretchers; elegant.
$2,350.00.

OCCASIONAL TABLE/STAND
Mahogany; flared gallery sides for depressed top with an apron of applied carvings forming annulet rings separated by geometric lines; curved sides on lower shelf. (Might have been used to display expensive bric-a-brac or delicate pottery.) 28"h x 19"dia top. $290.00.

PARLOR/CENTER TABLE
Mahogany; oversize bobbin or ball turnings; (one of the styles loosely attributed to the Elizabethan Revival, although few manufacturers were accurate with the furniture characteristics of that particular period); round double-layered top; generous lower shelf. Might have kept the Family Bible conveniently at hand as well as a Stereopticon with its box of views. 28½"h x 23"dia top. $375.00.

OCCASIONAL/ BEDSIDE TABLE Golden oak with brass fixture; the two front drawer sides are factory dovetailed while the two back corners are mortised and then wood pinned in the old way adapted from carpenters. Spool turnings; chamfered overhang top with angel-wings offset form the frame corners. 30"h x 17½"w x 16"dp. $345.00.

PARLOR TABLE/STAND Original marble top is missing; wood left is stained; pine and poplar; inverted bellflower finial on short round ballbased center joiner for legs. 28½"h x top 25½"w x 18½"dp. $195.00 as is.

PARLOR TABLE/DESK

Ca. 1870; mahogany with heavily applied gilded brass; Rococo Revival influenced; inlays; knees of the cabriole legs with ormolu covered feet are a well defined Goddess type face; flower circles on the hair while feathers grace the crowns; each has ruffled medieval breast protector and base insignias; note the ladies' pursed lips. Outlining the top and corners of the table as well as the apron sides are lavish patterns; keyholes at two side-front drawers could have been locked (the key is missing). 31"h x 67"w x 36"dp. $2,600.00 up.

TRAY with CANDLE SNUFFER & WICK TRIMMER COMBINED
Ca. 1840; toleware in black with a cameo-type handpainted lady's head and bust in vivid colors at the top of lacy handles; the sharp scissors were pushed together, snipping off burnt threads of a candlewick, they dropping into the colorfully painted tray which also had a "rest" for the tool. The scissors' edges were in regular usage as a candle snuffer. Tray 9'l x 4"w. $245.00.

KITCHEN, BAKER'S, or
POSSUM BELLY worktable.
Maple and poplar ca. mid-
1800's; two deep bins and
shallower drawers above all
have polished solid brass
pulls — both the right side
drawer and bin with sec-
tion dividers; two pullout
boards for rolling pastry
doughs, or whatever...top is
worn satiny smooth from
age and use; all four
squared legs have extended
turnings on ball-and-shoe
feet; there are strengthening stretchers for front and
back posts each side, and a
reeded valance at each end
below the overhang sur-
face. 28¾"h x 42"w x 27½"dp.
$795.00.

GAME TABLE
Ca. 1840's; Empire substyle;
front burl inlay panel; brass
hinges; walnut. 29"h x 36"w x
18"dp. $450.00.

GAME TABLE
Dark walnut with lighter burl applied; brass hinges permit top to be lifted and slid into playing position; dots outlining base on bracket feet. 29"h x 17"dp closed. $595.00.

Dealer tagged: "SOUTHERN GAME TABLE"
Walnut; teardrop brass pull on dovetailed drawer; checkerboard playing surface in a wide slightly slanted mortised corners frame; turned and squared post on S-curved legs. 30'h x 20'sq top. $265.00.

GAME TABLE
Mahogany; early Victorian; roundels on base scrolls of lyre style post (during his long career as a cabinetmaker, retiring ca. 1840, Duncan Phyfe of New York City used brass tubes, as in this table, in many furniture pieces); reeding and fluting; brass hardware; the inside well was for game accessories; brass animal feet terminate the legs. 30"h x 29¼"w x 15"dp. $325.00.

LIBRARY TABLE

Mahogany; a long drawer on only one side is opened by placing the fingers under the base of the drawer; both the top of the table and inside of the drawer are veneered; a distinctive pierced urn pedestal sits on a thick in-curved base with attached hairy lion's paw feet with prominent toenails; suggesting an Empire transitional, it reaches into "Grand Rapids Renaissance." 29"h x 60"l oval x 40" at widest center. $1,245.00.

144

PARLOR (CENTER) TABLE
French influenced; mahogany with painted top and four deep apron sides; while the decorating has aged, the rich colors still glow from the skillful old way of painting; in the garden setting, the romantic pair wear garments of the era; delicate slim legs have ornate toed animal feet. 29⅞"h x 30"dia top. $575.00.

PARLOR TABLE

Rarity, type customarily kept in the center of a room; a 1"dp white veined dark green marble top is deeply etched with a 2" wide border of hearts on a geometric background; a star center is surrounded by truly beautiful sprays of wild flowers, pods, buds, and leaves; a big turned ball tops the carved urn with teardrop bands and petals for its flare rim, all based on a 3-way thick wood base resting on curly-feathered lion's claw feet and a scrolled ankle. 28"h x 38½"top dia. $975.00.

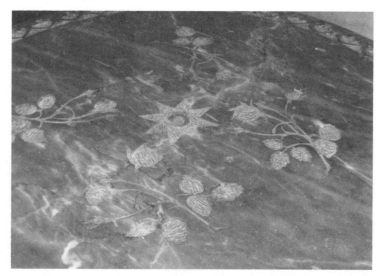

PARLOR/CENTER TABLE
Ca. 1880; walnut; grotesque bronze gargoyles decorate and strengthen with lions' heads on pad bases — a style not often seen; finger grooved and rope edge apron is below an overhang top; thoughtfully sized lower shelf. 29½"h x 30"sq top. $895.00.

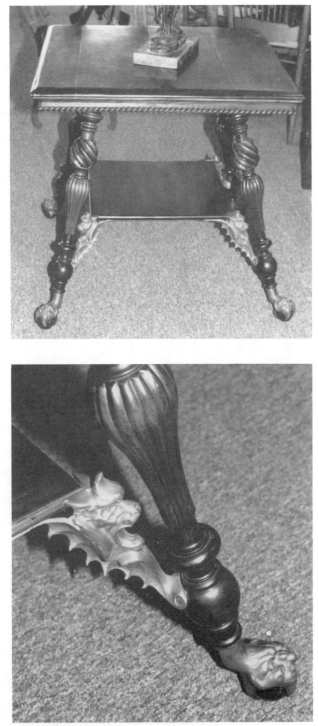

PARLOR TABLE
From late 1800's into turn of the century; mahogany; top has a mint-condition leather inlay with gold-scrolled outline; acanthus leaves on the knees and claw-and-glass-ball feet on the cabriole legs; 22"sq top overhangs rolled apron; large lower shelf. 28"h x 18½"sq shelf. $495.00 each — a pair.

TABLE
Mahogany; serpentine top and shelf edges; the large ball (bobbin) turnings of Elizabethan Revival are from about mid-century; again the very large higher valued brass claw and glass ball feet; shelf. 30"h x 27½"sq. $395.00.

PARLOR/ CENTER TABLE Ca. 1880's; walnut; turtle shaped top; flutings; short 4-parts high turnings with finial centering the pierced legs; inverted finial base. 30"h x 32"w x 22"dp. $750.00.

PARLOR/CENTER TABLE
Ca. 1880's; spool turned shaft with four fancifully shaped legs; seen at a huge outdoor once-a-year special antiques dealers' exhibit on Lake Ontario frontier. 30"h x 36"oval. $250.00.

PARLOR TABLE
Walnut; Eastlake lines with white and grey veined marble overhang top; reeding and flowers impressed on apron; balls and rings turned shaft with an inverted finial centering four step-cut and impressed flowers on the splayed legs below straight posts; burl inlays. 28"h x 28"w x 18"dp. $695.00.

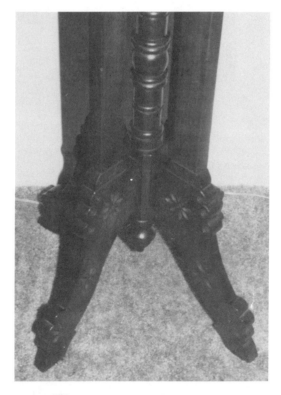

PARLOR TABLE

Walnut; white and light gray veined marble surface; one dovetailed drawer with a rose center brass pull and escutcheon; lyre base supported by an edge cut base and heavy legs. (Lyre styles were very popular during the Federal period.) 29½"h x 19"w top x 15"dp. $795.00.

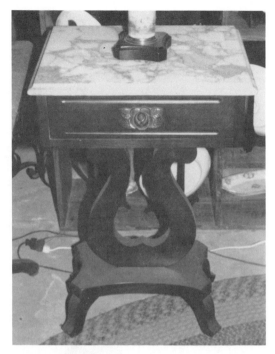

PARLOR TABLE

Ca. 1890; dropped stick and ball apron; spool and button turnings; stretchers center joined with a round wooden centerpiece having a mosquetop-like finial; wooden legs fits into round open top brass claw and glass ball legs and feet. 29½"h x 24"sq top. $445.00.

151

PARLOR TABLE

About 157 yrs. old; found in northeastern Maine; it was in the same family's possession for the entire time; the regional priest used to go to the home and say mass for all the folks roundabout, using this very table. An original cup (as shown here) was set at the base legs joiner, held firm with a dowel pin. White and gray veined marble top. It has only ever had one coat of clear lacquer. (Certainly historical Americana from the 1800's.) 29"h x 23"w x 16"dp. $950.00.

PARLOR TABLE

White marble top on walnut with a burl inlay on either side; pierced splayed legs with a turned center post having at base an inverted finial; white china casters. Typically Victorian, these tables were made in such vast quantities by so many manufacturers, they have survived for today's searchers more than any other furniture items from the nineteenth century with the exception of side chairs. 31"h x 21"w top x 16"dp. $675.00.

PARLOR TABLE Renaissance Revival substyle in black walnut with pale green and white veined marble top; finial at joining of the four fluted legs with an inverted one at the underside. 28½"h x 22"w x 17"dp top. $425.00.

PARLOR TABLE Eastlake influence; walnut; base turnings with large finials; incisings; casters. 27½"h x 29½"w x 21½"dp. $385.00.

PARLOR TABLE
Walnut; patterned incised apron; fretwork, reeding, and turnings on center wide stretcher with unusually large diameter end posts and finials holding firm four dramatically cut legs. 27¾"h x 29½"w x 21½"dp. $285.00.

WORK (SEWING) STAND/TABLE

These tables were more in the category of parlor pieces where ladies occupied themselves with "fancy work." Walnut; stick and ball with scallop trim; brass hinged lift top; note the unusual casters placement, at the end of the curved feet rather than under; cloth bag that held sewing supplies, small mending items, and such has been renewed, closely to the original flowered pattern. 30"h x 20"sq top. $175.00 (on a red sales tag).

Bags were often made from leftover fabrics — sometimes dress brocades, sometimes satin, embroidered by the worker. Until prices escalated, silk or taffeta sewing aprons were proudly embroidered and worn by the ladies. It is said needlework fashions show our cultural advancements as does furniture. A Bethlehem, Pennsylvania, Moravian school taught young ladies embroidery, emphasizing the weeping willow which depicts memorials and mourning.

FORMAL ARMCHAIR

Ca. 1877; mahogany; self wood and applied carvings; original upholstery in fine condition although arms are worn; scary lions' heads with open mouths are finials; mother-of-pearl and light wood inlays; an expensive motif — Grand Rapids makers were active in this medium while Leon Marcotte was famous for it in New York City; not confined to one revival period — included among many are Gothic, Renaissance, Rococo, and Sheraton characteristics; special inlays were oftentimes done by skilled cabinetmakers especially hired for such work. 39"h x 24"w seat x 33"dp x 15"fl. $425.00.

FORMAL ARMCHAIR
Ca. 1830; mahogany
with lighter wood,
gilt, and shell inlays
on shaped headpiece;
crimson silk reuphol-
stery to the original
pattern; fluting;
applied molding with
scrolls; shield splat;
many curved lines;
concave knees. 38"h x
24"w seat x 24"w at frt
x 20"w at bk x 16"fl.
$598.00.

FORMAL ARMCHAIR
Ca. 1865–70; Louis XVI
Revival; gilt and uphol-
stery restored; acanthus
leaves, tendrils, and open
rose applied carvings;
reedings; flutings. 36"h x
seat 22½"w frt x 17½"w bk
x 14"fl. $795.00.

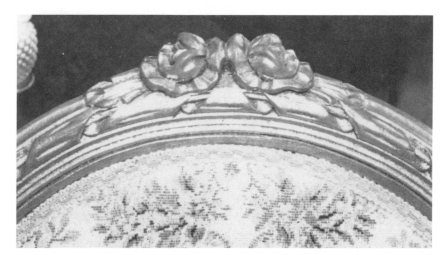

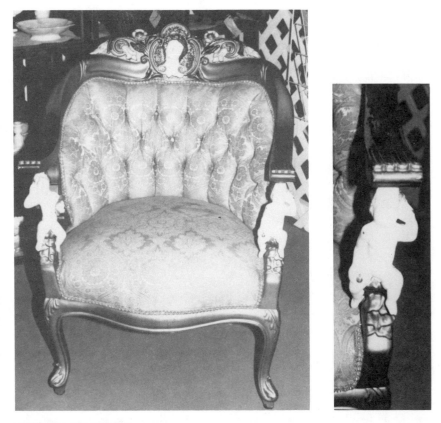

FORMAL ARMCHAIR

Ca. 1850; mahogany; silk brocade seat and tufted back, both gimp-edged; applied embellishments of acanthus leaves, fanciful pediment of white-painted bellflowers and other florals, and the crest of C-scrolls, beading, and more framing the painted woman's head and bust, her hair being black; a white cupid-like figure sits under each arm at post-top; cabrioled legs on spade-type pads. 39"h x 26½"w frt x 28½"w bk seat that is 20"dp and 17" from the floor. $875.00.

ARMCHAIRS
Rococo of Louis XV in overall finest quality gilt on wood; reupholstered to the original black crushed velvet with bronze pins; (in the 1850's Herter Bros. and Leon Marcotte of New York City were active in these French Revival furniture pieces); medallion splats having the same ornate embellishments in cherubim heads, the crest a profile with windblown hair (like crashing waves); self and applied carvings of innumerable designs; large half-roundel knees of cabriole legs having similar small rounds on the scrolled feet sitting on casters. 49½"h x 23½"w x 20"dp each chair. $1,500.00 the pair.

ARMCHAIR

Gilt on wood; well padded floral brocade arms and pillow back; reeded short spindle columns with lines repeated in the legs based on wooden casters; ribbon tied sheaf of wheat crest; finials; Louis XVI Revival whose fastidious characteristics moderated Louis XV's styles. 33"h x 28½"w x 21"dp. $525.00.

ARMCHAIR

Ca. 1930; shown here to illustrate how our modern makers have in turn borrowed from Victoriana just as the nineteenth century builders copied motifs from the eighteenth and seventeenth centuries; here the Louis XVI Revival style is done in green painted wood with needlepoint upholstery. 36"h x seat 23"w x 19"dp x 14"fl. $425.00.

PARLOR ARMCHAIR

Ca. 1885; Empire influence in mahogany; reupholstered; shaped splat with differences in border carvings on the top section; serpentine-crested headpiece with a girl's head at each corner; (note the eyes on one side look straight out — on the other the eyes have an upward right glance); animal feet. 38"h x 26"w at arms x seat 23"w x 20"dp x 13"fl. $425.00.

ARMCHAIR
Mahogany; ca. 1885–90; new
tapestry; shield back, overall
serpentine lines; floral crest.
39"h x seat 20"w x 18½"dp.
$785.00.

ARMCHAIR Shown for interest
Ca. 1920; "what goes around, comes
around," and in the continuing general
revival of Victorian decor, the good
endures. In walnut, vivid upholstery and
whorl feet terminating cabriole legs;
modern carvings as here show the influence of Rococo from John Henry Belter,
known for his laminated pieces and that
his chairs did not have a center back
seam. 56"h x seat 25"w frt x 21"w bk x
22"dp x 15"fl. $995.00.

ARMCHAIR
Ca. 1878; Eastlake style; red silk moire upholstery with wide gold gimp — this restored; incisings with shell crest; iron casters on front legs only. 37"h x 22"w back x seat 24"frt x 22"bk x 16"fl. $268.00.

PARLOR/ARM CHAIR
Colonial Revival in mahogany; new upholstery; applied carvings with a crest; floral and scroll seat supports and animal feet. 33"h x 30"w x 21"dp. $295.00.

ARMCHAIR
Walnut; Gothic crest over pierced splat; padded rose tapestry seat; iron casters. 36"h x seat 19"w x 18"dp x 13"fl. $325.00.

DEMI-ARMCHAIR
Stained brown tightly woven wicker on poplar; new eyecaning; double rows woven and braided act as the firming stretchers. 32"h x 18"w x 17"dp x 15"fl. $300.00.

ARMCHAIR
Solid cherry reupholstered; Colonial Revival in the Chippendale manner which Victorian factories (and some remaining cabinetmakers) began to produce after 1876 (often combined with Victorian ideas in decorating) when the public was restless for a "different look" in their furniture. 32"h x 21"w x 20"dp. $325.00.

ARMCHAIR
Mahogany; saddle seat; unusual styling with scalloped banisters; demi-arm handrests are mastiff heads with open mouths; also rare are the plain front legs while those at the back less widely splayed terminate at the floor with ball turnings; three turned stretchers; the headpiece is extra-high at center top. This was purchased in Georgia for office usage, and metal floor protectors were added. 36"h x 24½"w x 18¼"dp. $395.00.

CABANA (BEACH SHELTER) CHAIR

Tightly woven wicker seat for two, with wood, iron, and restored upholstery; pullout footrests; a waterproofed shield (here turned back over the top) protected the occupants from sun and wind when desired; these customarily hired at Victorian "watering places" carried on into the earliest 1900's — this from New Jersey's Atlantic City. 67"h x 47"w. $500.00.

CORNER CHAIR

Carried for usage into the nineteenth century from the latter 1700's, origin ca. 1770; fitting well into the nineteenth century with its heavily carved embellishments — only the stretcher wood has been left plain; faded and worn striped velvet upholstered slip seat; English oak in eclectic styling; urn fret-work and plain column slats; stepdown pediment. 30"h x 26"w x 19"dp seat x 16"fl. $2,500.00.

CORNER CHAIR
Ca. 1890; tagged "BRITISH BAM-
BOO CHAIR"; original natural reeds
stain; sometime during past 103
years the walnut seat was sparsely
padded and covered with narrow-
gimp-edged velvet; ball and button
turnings; careful continuity of simple patterns. 30½"h x 15½"sq x 17½"fl.
$255.00.

CORNER CHAIR
Ca. 1890; cherry; unusual style;
needlepoint seat cover once bril-
liant, still a bit colorful with florals and Roman gladiators at
center; spindles; large spool turnings; double stretchers all around
a mark of quality. 32"h x 18½"sq
seat x 15"fl. $335.00.

CORNER CHAIR

Cherry; Rococo Revival styling with center splat and pierced upright sides (reminiscent of Chippendale; he was attracted to Gothic themes, as is combined here with the Rococo); lighter applied carvings on the splat in various curls and other themes while that on the pediment verges on the "grotesque" in the face; this styling immensely popular in the 1800's as well as in the 1700's; wood casters. 31"h x seat 19"dia x 15"fl. $375.00.

CORNER CHAIR

Renaissance Revival; mahogany; red silk upholstered with thick padding; tufted backrest roll with ends of fluted scrolls; center turned post for carved wings and arcs cutouts; reeded band below those; fluted and (Eastlake-look fancy skirt valance); button feet; eclectic. 23"h x 24"dp. $475.00.

CORNER CHAIR
Ca. 1870, walnut; original
thick horsehair padding
under the brocade; wood
casters; reedings, turnings,
lion's paw foot front only;
tufted backrest and arms.
31½"h x 28"w frt seat x 26"dp.
$250.00.

CORNER CHAIR
Ca. 1870; mahogany;
needlepoint seat with
lilies center; bowed
back with a center
shield crest; brass cast-
ers. 28½"h x 28"w x
22"dp. $295.00.

PLATFORM ROCKER
Walnut; spring-action in iron fixtures; reuphol-stered; ponderous and comfortable; applied carvings and thick knuckle-rests; animal paw feet. 36"h x 22¼"w across back; 20"w seat x 20"dp x 8"fl. $395.00.

SHAKER ROCKING CHAIR
Ca. late 1800's; made at Mount Lebanon, New York; a 7-spindle back rocker with typically Shaker mushroom ends on the arms; rush seat; newspaper clipping shows very similar rocker and mentions "Shaker Museum, Old Chatham, New York." The back rocker extends 9¾". Seat 20"w x 17½"dp x 13"fl. $300.00.

The STOOL was not available but we were told it was in oak and pine, wood pegged, splayed legs with a stretcher at each longer side. 18"h x 19½"w x 11"dp. $85.00.

FOLDING ROCKER

Ca. 1870's; walnut; carpet fabric seat and back; these popular accent chairs; two curved slats at the top are incised, the headpiece having tiny balls; between the slats are fat-center turned spindles and a center of dainty jigsaw cutouts; note how stiles extend arms and thence on to be fastened on the outside of the rockers; at back the stiles are set into the rockers. Eastlake type. 31"h x 16"w seat x 16"fl. $800.00.

NURSING ROCKER
Poplar and maple; loop back Windsor; seven turned spindles and the two forming the V are the braces; partially ebonized; fluted loop; thick tightly woven rush seat; legs are socketed to the rockers. 30"h x seat 14"w x 12½"fl. $275.00.

ROCKING CHAIR
Walnut; restored brocade; framed back is a shield having a headpiece with a crest of petals and leaf curls at the sides; such low rockers were much used in many ways, one, for instance, in putting on ladies' slippers, sometimes of the style where ribbons were tied about the ankles. 41"h x 25" seat at its widest. $325.00.

SEWING ROCKER

Walnut; tapestry restored; folded flat for storage and easily brought out and set up when needed. 29½"h x seat 17½" x 17½". $185.00.

ROCKING CHAIR

Rod-back Windsor with Boston style headpiece; transitional — the crest developed from the Windsors; ca. 1840–50; usually categorized as a kitchen chair but while plain and comfortable and inexpensive they are as Victorian as the "Fancies"; even considered as a fireside rocker; slab seat still has its original mustard yellow paint, now almost faded out; an obliterated floral stencil on the crest; socketed legs; "carpet-cutter" narrow rockers. 29½"h x 15½"w seat x 14"fl. $175.00.

SIDE CHAIR
Kitchen loop-back Windsor type; ca. mid-1800's; poplar; seat rounded for body comfort. Each — 34"h x seat 15"w x 16"fl. $545.00 set of four.

ROCKING CHAIR
Unique high back style has been noted on an Ontario, Canada, chair about 1845, and again on one from the upper New York state/western New England area about 1875–80; seldom seen is the combination of five Windsor-type banisters with two plain lower slats, and a wide and a narrow crosspiece curved to fit the back of an occupant, woodpegged at each side to the round stiles; of mixed woods; the seat has been restored in a rough fabric; note the legs are set into thick rockers; teardrop finials, inverted. 45"h x 19"w x seat 17½"dp. $285.00.

ROCKING CHAIR
Mahogany; ladder or slat-
back; reverse arch curves;
ball and button turnings;
wide headpiece. 39"h x seat
21"w x 19"dp x 19"fl. $245.00.

ROCKING CHAIR
Mahogany; wide splat and down-
curved top slat; reupholstered
with brass head tacks holding
edges. 33"h x seat 20"w frt x 15"w
bk x 15½"fl. $225.00.

ROCKING CHAIR
Ca. 1870; mahogany; saddle seat; urn-shaped splat; scrolled knuckle rests; lion's paw feet on iron casters; chair has a heavy appearance. 35"h x 19"w bk x seat 23"w frt x 18"w bk x 16"fl. $548.00.

ROCKING CHAIR
Walnut armchair; purchased at Chicago's first World's Fair, the Columbian Exposition 1893; when the original upholstery was taken off for replacement, revealed was an attached metal plate with: "Patented by Hunzinger April 3, 1888"; stick and ball spindles with top 3½"dia and wheels at 2½"dia; mint green padded brocade seat; bowed apron; legs socketed into rockers; its 18½" seating height from the floor is unusual for this type rocker. 30½"h x 21"w. $625.00.
(George Hunzinger, a German immigrant, was famous 1850–1890 in New York City, advertising his "Fancy Chairs and Ornamental Furniture": eclectic themes that extensively incorporated wheels, cogs, pipes, spindles, ball and stick patterns, pistons, and knobs, for instance. This chair won a prize at the second Chicago World's Fair early in the 1900's. A rarity!

LADY'S ROCKING CHAIR
Cherry; slat-back with top one having center design; reupholstered; note finial size. 41"h x seat 16"w frt x 11½"w bk x 13"fl. $375.00.

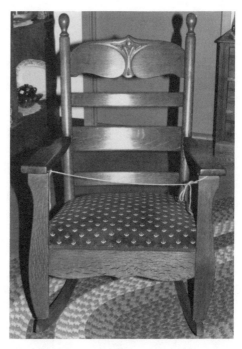

ROCKING CHAIR
Ca. late 1860's; stained wood and wicker, Wakefield style; delicate slats — note differences between lower and middle — and that most of the wood sections are wrapped, including the bulged posts and stretcher; two headpiece slats frame a center design, topped by a pediment of scallops; large mushroom finials; ball turnings; posts are set into narrow "rug cutter" rockers. 38½"h x seat 18"w front narrowing at the back x 15"fl. $375.00.

Cyrus Wakefield, a Boston grocer, experimented with reeds until beginning about 1865 he was able to produce rattan (and some wicker) furniture on wood frames.

ROCKING CHAIR

Ca. 1890; ebonized wood with lace tightly woven lace and floral wicker patterns as well as a band of more loosely woven Xs; five single reed verticals, demi-arms, and mushroom finials; Wakefield style. 33"h x seat 14"w x 18"dp x 15½"fl. $365.00.

BOSTON ROCKER

Ca. early Victoriana about 1840's; ebonized with gilt circled turnings and stenciled headpiece of fountain-like designs and tendrils; seven long spindles are bent to fit the headpiece; shallow saddle seat; legs socketed onto rockers. First produced in the cities, country makers later adopted these styles; real Bostons are considered transitional from the Windsors. 44"h x seat 29"w x 18¾"dp x 15"fl. $350.00.

BOSTON ROCKER
Ca. 1860's; headpiece style used after the 1840's, here with basic ebonized paint, striping and ball turnings in gilt; a fruit and floral stencil on top slat and at center of seat roll in yellow, gilt, and peach tones; six-spindle legs socketed onto rockers; the wave-like (cyma) curved seat first made customarily of pine in one piece, after the 1840's was made in three pieces, front and back additions attached to the flat seat portion. 35½"h x seat 15"fl. $350.00.

BOSTON ROCKING CHAIR
Characteristics of the Bostons but has an unusual caned seat; nicked ebonizing and the original brightly colored headpiece stencil with its cornucopia corner designs is almost obliterated; seven Windsor spindles; rolled front and back seat and center-curved armrests with under-rolled finger rests; dates early Victoriana. 42"h x 20"w x 17"fl. $395.00.

BOSTON SLIPPER ROCKER
Ca. 1860's; plank saddle seat; newly painted to the original...ebony base with gilt, umber, and more in nut and fruit patterns with corner cornucopias. The first Boston chair is sometimes attributed to Lambert Hitchcock of Connecticut in the late 1820's — and it has never been established why the chairs were called "Bostons" since they were made throughout our country. It is accurate to call those seen today as "Bostons-types." 35"h x seat 16"w frt x 14"w bk x 18"fl. $275.00.

ROCKING CHAIR

Ca. 1850; fiddleback type; rolled front and back seat typical of Pennsylvania's Boston Rocker; handfashioned; note irregularly cut sides of the splat; front post turnings; wood color differences of maple and pine construction and solid proportions; finger grip in oval crest. 40½"h x seat 20½"w frt x 17"w bk x 19"dp x 14½"fl. $495.00.

ROCKING CHAIR

Walnut; eye caning restored; inverted acorn finials — note the base of one of the stiles has a small iron strip mend firming the upright to the seat, so the chair has had some wear; the top curved slat has applied garland carvings while the lower has a rose center with moldings; bulged and turned spindles; note different looking oblongs fastening the underarm posts to the seat front. 39½"h x seat 17"w x 15"fl x 18"fl. $285.00.

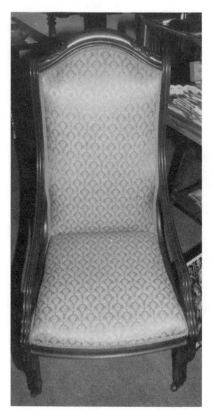

FORMAL SIDE CHAIR
Mahogany slipper chair with gilded crest; new gold patterned brocade upholstery; deep flutings; casters. 30"h x 10"fl. $495.00.

FORMAL CHAIR
Mahogany; ca. 1880; customarily a foyer piece; new fabric; reedings, flutings, heavily carved wide front stretcher with large knees on cabriole legs with whorl feet; crest at broken pediment balances stretcher pattern. 49"h x seat 21"w frt x 17"w bk x 17½"dp x 17"fl. $295.00.

FORMAL SIDE CHAIR

Walnut; new fabric; applied moldings; paw feet, carved knees. 34"h x seat 15"w frt x 14"w bk x 14½"dp. $375.00.

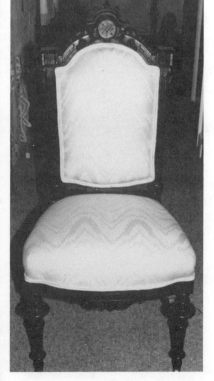

FORMAL SIDE CHAIR

Ca. 1890; walnut; Eastlake style; silk moiré reupholstered; trumpet legs on casters; cutout top with crest on broken pediment; incisings and squared stile tops. 41¼"h x seat 20"w frt x 15"w bk x 17½"dp x 18"fl. $400.00.

SIDE CHAIR
Walnut; for the parlor; moiré silk reupholstered over spring padding; applied carvings and winged S-pieces offset stiles; Eastlake type; casters. 38"h x seat 18"w frt x 13"w bk x 12"dp x 13"fl. $245.00.

FORMAL SIDE CHAIR
Walnut; Eastlake style; red
plush in plain and button-back;
incisings; wood and applied
carvings; inlays on top slat and
skirt valance; reedings; cutout
scallops below headpiece arch;
unusual whorl stile finials;
ornate front legs, plain at back;
wood casters; probably added
after its original construction is
a glue-held gimp-edged plush
round; on the arm it might have
been a convenient pincushion
— or might have been put on
back to keep walls from being
marred in a family addicted to
pushing or tilting back chairs.
37"h x seat 18"w x 17"dp; added
ball is 3"dia. $275.00.

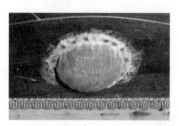

FORMAL SIDE CHAIR
Ca. late 1800's; walnut; green and white brocade; incisings on the applied pediment with a sausage roll crest; demi-arms; casters on front feet only — often so made; winged stiles. 37½"h x seat 13"fl. $195.00.

SIDE CHAIR (on left)
Walnut; Rococo style balloon back; tapestry reupholstered;
stayrail with a blossom, leaves, and scrolls while the crest
centered between pierced sides is a large bunch of applied
grapes in a basket hanging from a short branch along with
leaves and incisings; cabriole legs — said to be the first style
legs the factories attempted to reproduce. 34"h x seat 18½"w
frt x 17¼"w bk x 18"fl. $385.00.

SIDE CHAIR (on right)
Walnut; Rococo style balloon back; serpentine curved with
applied flutings; pointed stayrail; demi-arms gracefully high
attached to the back served to strengthen it; also kept ladies'
bustle skirts of the period, and hoops just prior to that, within
bounds. Considered to be the most popular style chair of the
mid-1800's, balloon backs were not pressed (laminated) but
made of solid woods; since they were made and sold by factories in almost every town of any size all over the country, it is
impossible to attribute them to a specific maker or area
unless they have a label or some mark of identification. 38"h x
seat 17½"w frt x 17"w bk x 21"dp x 17"fl. $385.00.

SIDE CHAIR
Ca. 1850's; balloon curved in Rococo
Revival style with red velvet tufted
upholstery; repairs; wide front cabriole legs, plain ones at back; walnut.
35"h x seat 15"w frt x 17"dp. $165.00.

SIDE CHAIR
Rococo Revival balloon back; reupholstered; applied broken pediment,
arched stayrail, and animal toes at the
base of balloon sides where attached
to chair seat back. 33"h x seat 14"w frt
x 13"w bk x 16"dp. $225.00.

SIDE CHAIR
Ca. 1890; Rococo substyle balloon back; needlepoint seat; shaped wide splat; curved top and lower slat; applied factory carvings. 34"h x seat 16"w frt x 12½"w bk x 16"dp x 17"fl. $245.00.

SIDE CHAIR
Ca. 1890; balloon back Rococo Revival style; carved crest, turnings, and caned seat; walnut. 34"h x seat 17½"w frt x 15"w bk x 15"dp x 16"fl. $225.00.

SIDE CHAIR

Walnut; an early Victorian little chair once "up there with the best of them" — now reduced to a bargain price status because it has two large underside back repairs inexpertly done; turnings include two oval slats, front stretcher and legs, the front with sausages; commodious newly caned seat; still sturdy and could be an accent chair not in regular usage. 31½"h x seat 17⅛" at widest part x 16⅛"dp. $45.00 as is.

SIDE CHAIR

Birch; rod-back; ca. 1860's; pressed vines design with acorn stiles finials; turnings. 35"h x seat 14½"w x 13½"dp x 17½"dp. $95.00.

192

SIDE CHAIR

From Connecticut, Lambert Hitchcock's "fancy" chair, originally bright with gold leaf, painting, and stenciling, through age and usage is now faint and dim. An eagle on a globe graces the middle slat while the mixed woods (could be hickory, ash, maple, even oak, two or more combined) are painted black; the rush seat has one side-middle split; typical are the back-curved stiles; from his shop at Hitchcocksville, Hitchcock shipped many chairs to buyers ordering from great distances over the country. 34"h x seat 17¾"frt x 15½"w bk x 15½"dp x 18"fl. $145.00.

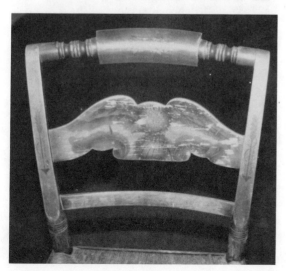

SIDE CHAIR
Ca. 1835; Hitchcock; the traditional black painted on mixed woods with gold leaf; bright colored stencils in fruit and leaf patterns; new rush seat to the original; handgrip crest and turnings. 34½"h x seat 17"w frt x 14"w bk x 14½"dp x 17"fl. $275.00.

SIDE CHAIR (one of eight)
Ca. 1835–40; Hitchcock manner with rush seats; handgrip; pierced center slat; convex front stretcher; (the small-ball-base tapered legs often seen on early Sheraton chairs); maple wood with stencilled patterns and gilded striping. (Solid wood seats following the earlier ones of woven rushes were in turn replaced with caning.) 34"h x seat 17½"w frt x 15"w bk x 16"dp x 18"fl. $3,500.00 set of eight.

SIDE CHAIR
Eastlake style; walnut; new caning; demi-arms with fluting; reedings; floral crest with incisings; spool and button trimmings. 33½"h x seat 17½"w frt x 13"w bk x 16"dp x 17¾'fl. $215.00.

"KITCHEN" SIDE CHAIR
Stained poplar ca. mid-1800's; Pennsylvania characteristics although used everywhere in our country; note flattened arrow spindles 7½"l; wide slats; semi-rolled front of the shaped seat. 34½"h x seat 16½"w frt x 14½"w bk x 14½"dp. $125.00.

SIDE CHAIR
Very old; waxes finish on maple; reflects Victorian Country Chippendale in the pierced shaped splat and the curved top slat; tightly woven rush seat; wood pegged construction. 39"h x seat 19"w frt x 15"w bk x 15"dp x 17½"fl. $215.00.

Shown for interest in what we would call "MODERN ECLECTIC" SIDE CHAIR
Mahogany; newly upholstered; ca. 1920; the grace of these lines from Queen Anne in Colonial Revival dispels any feeling of plainness. Each chair — 39"h x seat 18½"w frt x 16"w bk x 18"fl. $900.00 for a set of six — a number not easily found now.

SIDE CHAIR

"Cottage" style borrowing from the Boston type headpieces; dark stained poplar; tightly woven caned seat; spool turnings — one of the ways in which makers turned out hundreds of these informal, less expensive seating items for people of moderate means. 34"h x seat 15½"w frt x 12¾"w bk x 17½"fl. $195.00.

SIDE CHAIRS

Ca. after 1860; birch with stain finish; turned spindles between scallops forming both slats; pointed saddle shaped seat with eye caning; in the moderately priced "Cottage" style of late Victoriana. 33"h x seat 16"w frt x 14"bk x 17"dp x 18"fl. $675.00 set of four.

SIDE CHAIR
Ca. 1875–1880; maple (birdseye most desired for this work) grooved and stained to imitate natural bamboo, this latter at the height of its popularity, being light in appearance, not easily susceptible to dust; pretty back treatment of splat with upright and slat pieces; note bamboo framing below the upholstery. 35"h x seat 16"w x 15"dp. $350.00.

STICK SIDE CHAIR
Ca. 1850–60; once admired and ordered by Thomas Jefferson; reflects the Windsor rod-back with Sheraton-type double slats; maple with a shaped hickory seat; with bamboo materials in furniture at its peak, painted grooves in turnings were clever and acknowledged imitations; among others, Philadelphia makers shipped their wares as patterns to local craftsmen all over the country. 37"h x 16½"w x seat 16"dp. $225.00.

198

SIDE CHAIR
Ca. 1875; stained poplar; stick and ball and ball turnings on slats; caned seat; bustle arms. 32½"h x seat 15"w frt x 14"w bk x 14½"dp x 17"fl. $125.00.

SIDE CHAIR
Ca. 1870; square Eastlake lines; stick and ball half-spindles, pressed head-piece design with finger grip crest; caned seat is new. 33¾"h x seat 16"w frt x 14½"w bk x 15½"dp x 17½"fl. $625.00 set of six.

SIDE CHAIR
Walnut; Renaissance styling (which covers a multitude of Revival characteristics); solid plank seat; headpiece and shaped stay-rail each fit into the stiles; very old. 32½"h x 17"w frt x 14"w bk x 14½"dp x 17"fl. $425.00 set of four.

SIDE CHAIR
Renaissance Revival style; stained maple with birdseye inlays; new caning; fretwork splat; widespread bustle arms; shaped seat; heavy spool turnings. 39"h x 22"w x 20"dp. $135.00.

SIDE CHAIR
Walnut; what was probably a cane
seat has been replaced with plywood;
applied molding on seat frame
dipped at front into an apron; large
grooved roundel centers the splat
while the crest is fluted and incised.
34"h x seat 17¼"w frt x 16½"dp x 18"fl.
$75.00.

SIDE CHAIR
Ca. 1890's, fancifully carved walnut with
incisings in a Renaissance manner;
reupholstered; burl inlaid center splat.
Each chair — 35"h x seat 18"w frt x 13"w
bk x 15"fl. $425.00 for set of two (remain-
ing from four).

SIDE CHAIR

Birch; ca. 1880; factory made and used during popularity of true "Country Chairs" so they were included in that category; stained birch; eye caning; short stick and ball turnings between top two slats. 32"h x seat 16"w frt x 13½"w bk x 16"dp x 17½"fl. $125.00.

SIDE CHAIR

Walnut; ca. 1870; factory made with country styling; demi-arms (bustle sides) with flutings; reedings; ball and spool with button turnings; stick and ball trims; tiny back of knees shaped apron; stiles are fanned out (or lightly splayed). The seat sags from years of usage — it could easily be recaned — or if you prefer, put a cushion on it. 34¾"h x seat 16"w frt x 14"dp x 18"fl. $75.00 each — three left from set of original six.

SIDE CHAIR

American walnut in the Renaissance manner; ca. 1870; reupholstered — but the gimp needs attention — three flattened arrow spindles between square ones having impressed roundels; applied leaf carvings on the lower slat spool-fastened to the stiles; stepdown top on thick scrolled demi-arms; the applied top rail with reedings and incisings projects farther on one side — more completely incised. Each chair — 35"h x 18"w x 17"dp. $975.00 for a set of four.

SIDE CHAIR
Poplar stained darker; splat an extended family relative of the fiddleback; "Grand Rapids Renaissance" eclectic; new caned seat; incisings and crest roundel; quality piece with the two front stretchers spool and button turned; curved demi-arms. 40"h x 17¾"w frt seat x 14¾"w bk x 18"fl. $675.00 set of four.

SIDE CHAIR
Factory-made in the late 1800's; almost every town of any size in our country during the nineteenth century offered these chairs for sale, made from local woods, not usually regional specialties; Eastlake style with spindle back, reeded top and bottom slats, and button turned stretchers and legs. 33"h x seat 15"w frt x 13½"w bk x 14"dp x 15"fl. $110.00.

DINING SET OF FOUR
CHAIRS and the TABLE
Picture of the table was not
available — only a glimpse
of the inlays on each
valanced side and one
chair as an example of the
four. Ca. 1850's; mahogany
in Rococo Revival style; cut
velvet fabric; carvings and
inlays were handfashioned
by skilled cabinetmakers;
fretwork; beading; fluting;
scrolls; and much more;
cabriole legs with scrolled
feet on pads; handsome
applied apron embellish-
ments. $3,600.00 the set of 5
pcs. Chair — 42½"h x 23½"w
x 19¼"dp seat. Table —
31½"h x 71"l x 43"w.

PARLOR SET (SUITE)
Ca. last quarter of the 1800's
with eclectic influences; both
heavy looking and delicate in
plain and flame (or crotch)
mahogany; brocade upholstery;
deeply grooved arms with scroll
ends topped with fluted curves;
C-curve cutouts on unusually
wide urn-shaped splats; open
mouth lions' heads with fero-
cious expressions project from
each side of the shaped headpieces; unique in fine quality
workmanship; great attention
overall and to detailing of carvings. $1,495.00 the set of 3 pcs.
Settee — 39"h x 40½"w x 20"dp
seat x 15"fl.
Armchair — 38"h x 22"w x
18½"dp seat x 15"fl.
Rocking Chair — 38"h x 22"w x
18½"dp seat x 15"fl.

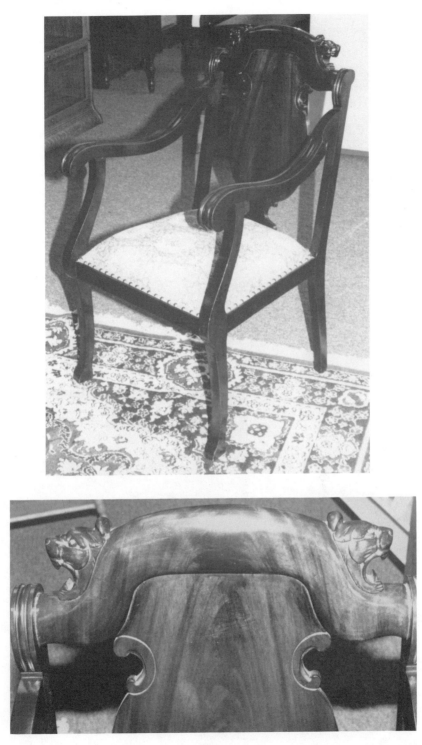

ARMCHAIRS seen at a gallery near Rome, Georgia, that had been among furniture used in the 1990 movie "Perfect Harmony"; both with new upholstery; mahogany.

Hoop back; deep carvings in the manner of the second French influence of Louis XVI. 42½"h x 26"w x 22"dp. $350.00.

Arms and posts deeply curved; cup and ball turned base legs. Renaissance characteristics. 39"h x 23"w x 21"dp. $325.00.

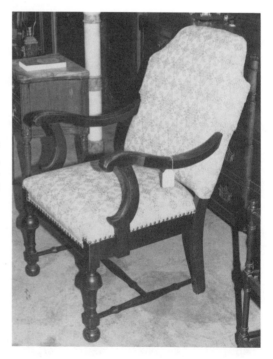

LADIES' AND GENTLEMEN'S PARLOR CHAIRS

Both chairs walnut; rose velvet covers a plain seat and tufted back over horsehair padding; Rococo Revival about 1860's; (a period gradually phasing out the Late Classical while retaining many of it's graceful lines, as balloon backs); deep grooved serpentines; although the applied crest on each chair has the same fruit, nuts, and leaves motif, the maker has assembled them in different positions; stubby legs on paw feet over iron casters. Ladies' (right) — 33"h x 22"w x 18"dp. $350.00. Gentlemen's (below) —38"h x 22½"w x 19"dp. $350.00.

PARLOR SET

Ca. late Victorian; Eastlake style; black walnut; large leaf scrolls in applied carvings; fluted bulbous-base posts under knuckle-arms on the settee and platform rockers; shield backs, brocade upholstery, and cutouts. In Sears' 1897 catalogue a similar set is offered as one of their "greatest bargains parlor sets" at a $75.00 price reduced to $47.00. $2,500.00 five pieces.

Settee — 38"h x 48"w x 21"dp x 17"fl.

Two platform rockers (each) — 36"h x 24"w x 19"dp x 17"fl.

Two side chairs (each) — 38"h x 20"w x 19"dp x 17"fl.

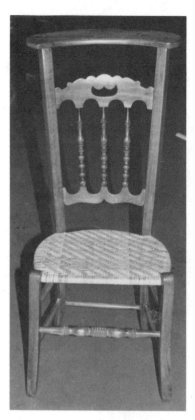

VALET CHAIR
Maple and birch; woodpegged 3½"w top slat; fit the shoulders of a suit-coat; new woven reed seat; splayed stiles and turned spindles; scalloped slats, the top one with a finger-hold; this general idea continued into modern forms still in popular usage. 39"h x seat 16"w x 14"dp x 15"fl. $195.00.

POTTIE CHAIR (CLOSESTOOL)
Ca. early Victoriana; ebonized with headrest typical Boston style; through age and usage the colors once bright are now muted; a long valance hides the chamberpot and at center is a liftoff round; tall Windsor-like spindles. 38"h x 21"w seat x 17½"dp x 16½"fl. $195.00.

POTTIE CHAIR
(CLOSESTOOL)

Ebonized (grain-painted) and stenciled; center knob permits lifting and removing center cover 11"dia — finger rests cut in; a deep valance conceals the chamberpot; Boston style of early Victoriana. 37½"h x seat 21½"w x 18½"dp x 16"fl. $225.00.

FOLDING THEATER SEAT/MISC. USAGE
Mixed woods pressed seat and back with reeded stands; mostly these were in connected sections of four seats each. 30½"h x seat 15"w x 17"dp x 16½"fl. $65.00.

OFFICE/DESK CHAIR
Mahogany; jigsaw back cutouts with applied scroll carvings; fancy brass cage around iron revolving mechanism that also permits being tilted back; heavy iron casters; turnings; and cut-down ledges arms. 41"h x seat 20"w frt x 17¼"w bk x 19"dp x 17¾"fl. $295.00.

CHILD'S CRIB
Ca. 1870; walnut; roundel on headboard, brass rosette fasteners on each post for low side boards; new white china casters. 41"h at crest x 53"l x 29"w. $845.00.

YOUTH'S BED
Ca. 1860; walnut; paneled head and base boards; fluted applied moldings. Headboard — 42"h x 37½"w. Footboard — 35"h x 37½"w. $1,500.00.

DOLL BED
Pine; stepdown cutouts on each of four posts; crosswise liftout slats hold padding; large headboard applied circle and four half-acorns each on head and baseboards. 36"l x 30"w. $85.00.

CHILD'S CRADLE
Mixed woods including maple, poplar, and walnut; one spindle missing; handfashioned; each of corner posts in a bow, from set in the rockers to holding the oxbow center-peaked tops; long slats are replacements. 29"h x 37"l. $125.00.

DOLL CARRIAGE

Little Missy from Ohio, Atto C. Arnold (in this picture she was 5 years old), out for a stroll with her doll in its carriage in 1891. Stroller made of hard maple with iron handle shafts and blackened iron spring-based frame; wooden wheels. Value for the carriage only $350.00– $425.00.

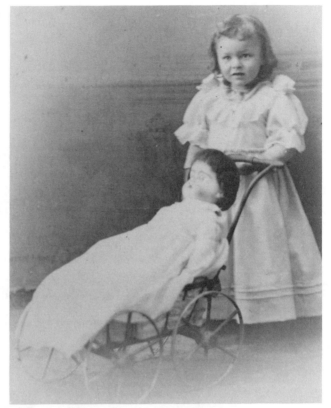

DOLL CARRIAGE

Wicker with iron and wood frame; spring action; umbrella type parasol hung from bar could be opened to shade the doll; padded cloth lining removable for laundering. 22"h x 22"l x 9"w. $395.00.

DOLL CARRIAGE
Typically Victorian, fancifully made in many patterns from wicker, wood, and iron; a life-size doll is all ready for a push-stroll. Note single reed strands forming curved sides and foot of the buggy. No price — museum quality.

DOLL CARRIAGE
Rare use of porcelain enamel on body; wicker, cloth, and iron fixtures and spring base; white painted wood; rubber rim iron wheels; top can be folded down flat. Note handle shaft curls. 35½"h x 12"w x body 24"l. $300.00.

BABY CARRIAGE (STROLLER)
Underside labeled: "Heywood, The Walter Heywood Chair Co. Fitchburg, Mass." During 1885–1880, the factory sent out hundreds of catalogues advertising their furniture products. White painted wicker with the original gold corduroy lining; wood; iron fixtures — rubber rimmed wheels — underbody iron spring action; fancifully fashioned with adjustable lie-back and let-down foot for letting a sleepy baby lie flat — or making the ride more comfortable as little legs grew longer; black enameled handle grip. 43" full l x 32"h x 19½"w. $550.00.

CHILD'S CARRIAGE/ BABY BUGGY
Black stained wicker; body beige corduroy lined; iron fixtures with spring action on base; rubber tired wheels. $475.00. Rear offset wheels 16½"dia. Front offset wheels 12"dia.

CHILD'S PERAMBULATOR/CARRIAGE

Ca. 1850's, a very special conveyance used by parents of considerable means; wood, iron, and much gilt; down feathers inside pleated and tufted upholstery; the crushed green velvet has been restored and there is black enameling on parts including the wood wheels. The carriage was purchased at an auction by a dealer in Florida — various parts had weakened until the whole was offered in pieces. For the dealer to research the style and put it all back together as original took eight months. 43"h to canopy top x 51" overall length x 16½"w. $2,000.00.

CHILD'S STROLLER
White painted bentwood; closely woven reed seat; black iron and rubber rimmed wheels; stick and ball spindled back and underarms; all original with label underseat: The Walter Heywood Chair Co., Fitchburg, Mass. — "Heywood Bros. Co." 35"h x seat 14"w x 13"dp. $325.00.

CHILD'S CARRIAGE

Stitched black leather exterior, white lined; folding top is cracked with age; iron spring action base; rubber tired wheels. 29"h x 26"w x 32"l. $95.00.

TOY CUPBOARD/ CABINET

Walnut; handfashioned with random width back boards; 2 shelves inside; framed glass doors; china knobs and brass fixtures; mortised joining of reeded drawers; wavy gallery and apron; wide serving shelf. 28"h x 19¼"w x 10½"dp base x 6½"dp top. $350.00.

CHILD'S ROCKING CHAIR
Walnut; curved headpiece with one turned
stretcher; bentwood back flowing into the seat
is punched-out designs on three layers of
pressed wood; brass fasteners; an unusual
small chair. 20"h x seat 12½"w x 7"fl. $225.00.

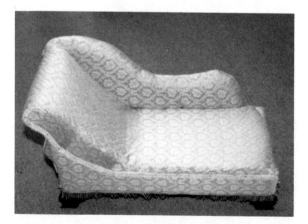

DOLL'S LOUNGE/COUCH
Wood frame covered with rose brocade upholstery;
bracket feet. 24"l x 11"w. $245.00.

CHILD'S SET
White painted wicker, all with braided borders. Thin
plain wood top. Closely woven reeds. Uncommon to
find these complete sets today. Generally speaking,
contemporary collectors prefer tables having wood
tops. Table — 16½"h x 17½"dia. Chairs (each) — 25"h x
20"l x 13"dp. $125.00.

YOUTH SIDE and ARMCHAIR
For both: ca. 1890; double bent hoop-
back; feathers, flowers, and curls
impressed into an overall design on
pressed paper seat; hickory. (Michael
Thonet, a Viennese, with his brothers
about 1850 on, became famous for
bentwood forms, shipping from Aus-
tria all over the world. In Wisconsin
the Sheboygan Chair Co. began to
duplicate these forms in the late
1800's.) Side Chair — 25½"h x seat
12½"dia x 12¾"fl. $125.00. Armchair —
24½"h x 13½"dia seat x 12"fl. $125.00.

YOUTH CHAIR

Ca. 1875; stained natural reeds color — wicker and maple; eyecaning on seat with serpentine front; widely splayed legs with stretchers, under-arm and under-seat braces were all done for firming; as wicker began gradually to replace rattan after 1885, a piece made from those reeds (usually white painted) had become a "must" in every home that could afford one; Massachusetts was among the supplying states. 35"h x 20"w. $250.00.

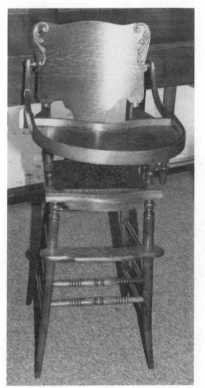

HIGH CHAIR

Maple; veneered back with applied S-scroll traceries; same curves on seat apron and footrest; turnings; substantial protected edge tray was lifted up and back over the head of the child — to hang down the back on pins; seat is restored pressed paper. 29½"h x 11"w x 10"dp. $395.00.

YOUTH CHAIR
Ca. 1840; for an older child and often called a "pullup to the table chair"; never had a tray; plank seat; ebonized and the headpiece re-stenciled to the original. 38"h x 17"w x 16"dp. $325.00.

YOUTH CHAIR
Ca. 1890; mixed woods; the hoop back is uncommonly caned (both that and the seat restored); bentwood forming the curved arms and arch; the curved edge seat, turned spindles and slightly splayed legs add grace; wide footrest; while similar to Windsor, not a true "Firehouse" chair. 39"h x 17"w x 16"dp. $345.00.

CHILD'S ROCKING CHAIR

Wicker pecan-brown stained; braided edges and wood framing and rockers. 30"h x seat 18"w at frt x 14"w at bk x 16"dp x 15"fl. $325.00.

CHILD'S ROCKING CHAIR

Ca. 1890's; very closely woven wicker with wide arms — overall braided edges; wood rockers and frame; open criss-cross back pattern; wicker furniture of the 1800's was tightly woven in attractive patterns; as 1900 approached, weaves became more loosely done and the styles much simpler. $250.00.

CHILD'S ROCKING CHAIR
Ca. 1850; ebonized wood with
brown painted arms, turnings on
front under-arm and leg posts;
Boston style after 1835 of characteristic headrest and rolled front
and back seat; stencils in gilt and
bright colors; four spindles. The
thin rockers with legs socketed
on, and general appearance indicate this might have been a converted straight chair. 30"h x
14½"w x seat 17'dp to top of roll.
$225.00.

CHILD'S ROCKING CHAIR
From Pennsylvania; ebonized
wood; stencil on top slat looks
more like an inquiring child has
rubbed to see what was underneath — rather than that it was
worn off through usage; three
spindles; top slat also seen on
Ohio pieces. 29"h x seat 18½"w frt
x 17½"w bk x 16½"dp. $195.00.

CHILD'S ROCKING CHAIR
Stained poplar; tightly woven
wicker with Boston style seat
rolled down at front; button
and ball turnings; note finials
on the stiles — stick and ball
among other back and crest
designs. 29¼"h x seat 16¼"w frt,
narrower at back, 10"fl.
$110.00.

CHILD'S ROCKING CHAIR
Ca. 1860; maple; new eye caning on seat and back; a few
curves "dress up" the simplicity. 25"h x seat 14"w frt x 12"w
bk x 14½"dp x 11"fl. $325.00.

CHILD'S ROCKING CHAIR
Iron and iron wire painted black;
new padded upholstery; S-scrolls.
29"h x seat 13"w x 14"dp x 12½"fl.
$135.00.

CHILD'S ROCKING CHAIR
Plain and quarter sawn oak;
fancy Victoriana with its serpentine seat front, pierced pressed
plywood center, cutout portion
of tall splat, turnings, knuckle
arms scrolls, wood carved and
applied, and the different than
usual spool and ball turned stile
tops. 29"h x seat 14"w frt x 13"w
bk x 16"dp. $125.00.

CHILD'S FOLDING CHAIR
Ca. late 1800's; carpet back and seat; large ball stile finials; roundels concealing demi-arms extending into the legs. (Doll is a friend of the family.) 23½"h x seat 10½"w x 11½"dp x 12"fl. $485.00.

CHILD'S TRUNK
About 100 years plus old; dome top; pine with
blackened iron fixtures; lift out sectioned tray;
paper picture of a girl with long curls still bright
with firm colors; wide leather handles. 9"h x 12"w x
7½"dp. $195.00.

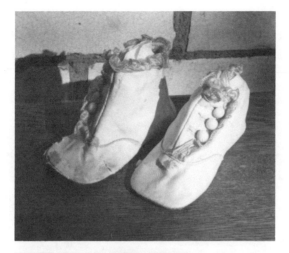

WHITE KID (LEATHER) SHOES
Typical little shoes from the nineteenth century
that may have been carried in such small
trunks. Ordinarily saved to be worn for dress
up occasions; difficult to find now, especially in
such good condition even with all the original
silk-covered buttons remaining; pale rainbow
colors in ribbon lace. Size still faintly visible in
the left shoe is 4½. $45.00 pr.

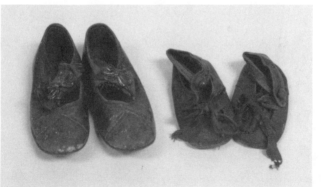

TWO PAIRS OF SHOES
The small pair is light brown with silver filigree butter-
flies on strap fasteners. Only the button under the strap
remains on one of the two scuffed-toed shoes. The larger
pair is the same color but ties with bows. No price —
museum quality.

A DOLL TRUNK

An early one from the 1800's; pine with iron banding and hardware, a wood strip ending in a fancy embossed brass triangle; leather handles; dome top; two-sectioned lift out tray. 11"h x 16"w x 9½"dp. $210.00.

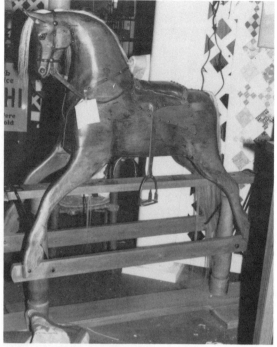

ENGLISH TRESTLE HORSE

Ca. 1880's; carved wood; restoration included wooden rocking base, glass eyes, iron and leather trappings, mane and tail; original body in excellent condition. Horse measurements only, 37"h x 43"l nose to tail. Rarity. $3,500.00.

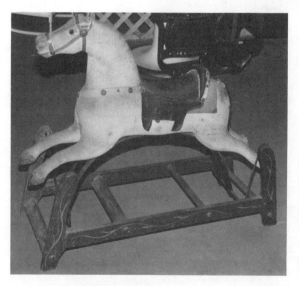

ROCKING HORSE

Seeing them in Christmas window displays, poorer children must have longed to have one; round iron back and forth rockers; all original brown cloth hide-covered wood body, black saddle, red painted wood base frame with mustard yellow touches, darker hooves, shoe button black eyes; energetic little riders left their traces in missing tail, ears, mane, and trappings. 32"h x 35"w x 15"dp. $575.00.

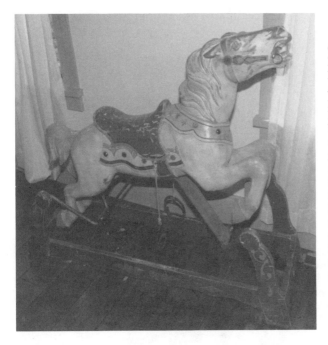

CHILD'S ROCKING/HOBBY HORSE
All original; white painted wooden horse on a red base, colorful gilt collar and red with yellow designs on saddle; leather trappings and iron fixtures — even has the bit in its mouth; expressive glass eyes; animal is handcarved with uncommon leg position. $1,200.00.

PULL TOY
Circus horse; carved wood lavishly painted in gold, green, black, white, red, and yellow; horsehair tail, leather saddle and blanket; Handfashioned in the 1890's; wood wheels and base. $875.00.

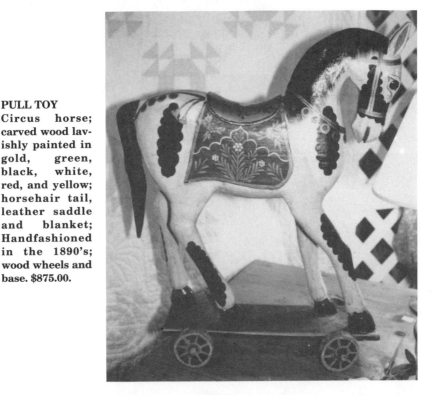

CHILD'S ROLLTOP DESK
Ca. 1880; walnut; rarely now
seen; carved wood pulls and
a knob to lift the roll; inside
are divided compartments;
lower shelf and a pullout
work/writing tray. 37"h x
24½"w x 15½"dp. $750.00.

FURNITURE OF REEDS

WICKER SET
Three pieces in white painted wicker and wood; closely woven reeds of the mid-to-late-1800's when first manufactured in this country; its cool-looking and airy structures particularly favored in our southlands. Reinforced splayed table legs; both chairs are rockers with wide arms. Table 26½"h x 31½"dia. $895.00 set.

PORCH SWING
Hung by chains; white painted wicker and wood of the tightly woven reed styles of the 1800's; patterned high back, openwork below that and along the sides; braced arms. 57"l x seat 22"dp. $725.00.

ROCKING CHAIR
White painted wicker and wood; a handsome,
closely woven piece with the arms ending in huge
finger-rest circles; new cushion. 34"h x 22"w x seat
20½"dp. $150.00.

Although there are still fine originals left to be
found, broken wicker parts are extremely difficult
to repair; there are extensive reproductions.

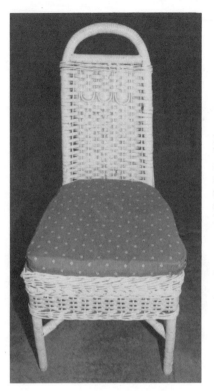

DESK CHAIR
Wicker and wood with a new upholstered removable seat pad; braid and
crest half-circles with an open arc carrying space; reed-wrapped legs and
stretchers. 35½"h x seat 16"w frt x
16½"dp. $95.00.

BEACH CHAIR

Wood and wicker lightly brown stained; seat half lifts up for storage space underneath; leather feet; hinged to fold flat; two sets of leather straps keep chair fastened flat when carried by the open space handhold at the back top. Seat and back each 17½"w x 19"dp. $95.00.

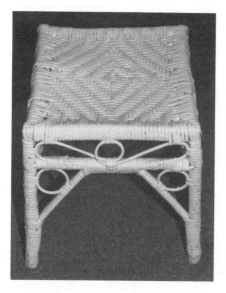

FOOTSTOOL
Wicker on wood frame; seat design woven in a diamond pattern while single reeds are decoratively curled on the undersides. 11"h x 13"sq. $45.00.

SEWING CABINET
Ca. 1890; storage basket with domed lid; dished bottom lower shelf; white painted wicker and wood with a no-harm small restoration at a handle joining; widely splayed legs with unusual wrapped bulges and tiny balls at their bases; carrying handle. Customarily taken into the ladies' parlor; having had fine needlework stored in the cabinet, the pieces could be taken out for dainty stitching when guests came to chat — or for mild occupation at the owner's leisure moments. 28"h x 13½"sq top x 6"sq shelf x 6"fl. $375.00.

SEWING CABINET
Cloth lining inside painted wood and wicker sides with a metal bottom in the well; carved wood knob for the hinged lift top; braided trims and splayed feet; two carry-about loops; wood shelf below. 26¾"h x 14¾"sq top. $225.00.

MORTUARY BASKET

Tightly woven and dark stained wicker
with a cloth covered wood bottom
(above); lid (below); the basket has
leather straps for carrying; today it
hangs on a wall with artificial flowers
decoratively arranged inside — and no
indication of its original purpose. 76"l x
21"w. $450.00.

PLANT STANDS
White painted wood and wicker; ca. mid-1800's; the four wood uprights also extend to form the acorn shaped feet; inside near the top is a wood platform to hold the pot of plants. Top dia 12½" x base 15"sq. $200.00 the pair.

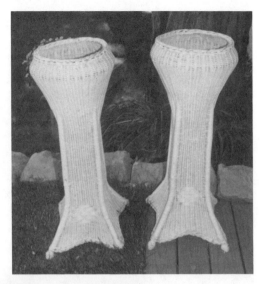

PLANT STAND
Loosely woven wicker white painted, the weave years later than the closely woven styles earlier in the nineteenth century; wood legs extending from the top are splayed below a wood shelf. 31"h x 12"dia top. $125.00 stand only.

PLANT STAND
White painted wicker and wood; braces, wrapped wood sections. (Probably had a metal liner). 23½"h x 17"w x 23½"l. $150.00.

PLANT STAND
Wrapped and painted wood and wicker with a tin liner. (Pots of greenery and begonias.) 30½"h x 28"w x 11¾"dp. $150.00 stand only.

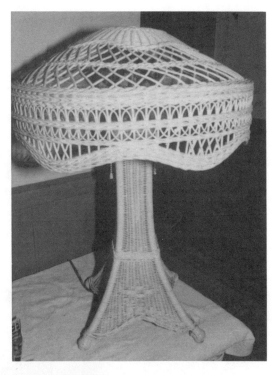

TABLE LAMP
Closely woven white painted wood and wicker; braid edge of scallops on designed shade; has been electrified. 25"h x 11"sq at base. $225.00.

ROCKING CHAIR
Wicker and wood white painted; reupholstered as originally done; widely splayed arms. 37"h x seat 19"w x 18"fl. $275.00.

FLOOR LAMP
Wood and wicker white painted, tightly woven, and handsomely designed; these, along with many other reed pieces, were extensively purchased by Victorians for their sun porches and "cottages" (many cottages were luxurious homes); today they are being sought by home-makers and decorators. 68"h x 17"dia base; shade 29"dia. $350.00.

FLOOR LAMP
A crown design on this tightly woven white painted early wood and wicker lamp. 65"h shade x 26"dia. $325.00.

BOX
All original; wood base covered with wallpaper (perhaps why dealer called this their "wallpaper box") on which, after more than a century, the patterns are still evident in many places; thin black iron fixture; articles appearing on the newspaper lining are dated 1842. $550.00.

LAP DESK
Early Victorian; black stained wood; a separate middle hinged left becomes a flat writing surface when set between the base and the lid; five divided compartments in the base for ink bottle, pens, pencils, and such while paper could be kept in the long section. Originally, it could have been locked. $275.00.

LAP DESK

Ca. 1879–80; black grain-painted with bright colors including red and yellow inlays; white and blue enamels; mother of pearl insets. Has the original brass key. Inside are thin stained wood separators for writing supply compartments. (The new stand is for display). 6"h x 16"w x 10"dp. $1,350.00.

BOOK BOX SAFE
Ca. early 1840's; found in New England and used for years in a Batavia, New York, home; of pine and basswood; covered with a varnish-like treatment accented for trimming with antique mustard-yellow coloring and a stamped center picture too faded to be discernible. Inside, a hollow space hid valuable papers, and sitting on a shelf among authentic volumes, the safe was indistinguishable. 7¾"h x 6½"w x 2¾"dp. $275.00.

TABLE BOX
Ca. 1870–80; walnut hand carved box and liftoff lid with two quail resting on grasses; leaf designs on four sides of the box and reeding on all edges. Original key. $395.00 plus.

BOXES FROM AN OBSOLETE SEWING MACHINE

Ca. 1880's. Three divided drawers each; these make great boxes for any room to hold all sorts of those elusive "things" hard to "find-a-place-for"; walnut wood with depressed circles, knobs, and deep groovings; beading on edges. One small lower length is broken away. 14½"h x 5"w x 14"dp. Six at $38.00 ea., two sets.

UTILITY BOX

Ca. late Victorian. Another part converted to practical usage from an obsolete highboy — one of the shelf-side parts; ebonized knob with finely incised design on center is thin brass; even base and sides of the drawers are walnut; factory scallops and pegs; dovetails. 5"h x 6½"w x 9"dp. $125.00.

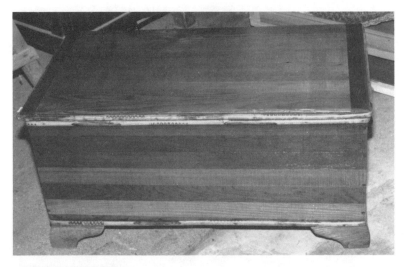

SHIRTWAIST TRUNK
Sometimes shortened to "waist" trunk. Ca. late 1800's into the turn of
the century; bamboo edges trim pine wood; wood handles; new paper
liner is a typical 1800's period pattern. 14½"h x 29½"l x 16"dp. $125.00.

LADIES' SHIRTWAIST TRUNK
The larger of the two sizes shown herein; flat pine top with bamboo trim. Used to store and/or carry waists during the late 1800's into the earlier 1900's. (Birdseye maple often used to simulate natural bamboo.) 15"h x 30¾"l x 18"dp. $145.00.

DOME TOP TRUNK
Ca. 1850–60; an all original "Jenny Lind" style trunk; impressed designed leather covers the wood body; black iron strips with brass studs; flap over an iron escutcheon for a now-missing key; leather side straps; inside lift out tray and prettily colored (now faded) paper liner with a lady's picture on the underside lid. 17"h x 28"w x 16½"dp. $325.00.

DOME TOP TRUNK

Wood based trunk entirely covered with various wood strips having brass embossed end fasteners, blackened tin, and wide green painted tin panels fully embossed in patterns of flowers and leaves; a brass key keeper (key now gone) with iron strap latch; inside is a removable tray and a tiny floral-patterned paper liner almost aged white as is the once-brightly colored picture in lid center of a Victorian young lady; leather handles with brass fasteners. 19"h x 28"w x 14½"dp. $165.00.

FLAT TOP TRUNK

Late Victorian; pine body originally covered with canvas, which through the years became so badly travel-stained that dealers removed the cloth and restored the trunk to its natural wood; iron banding; the wood strips have brass teardrop ornamental fasteners; key now gone from brass lock and its escutcheon; the trunk's interior lid is lined with historically patterned paper as close to the original as our modern shops can provide. These styles continued well beyond the turn of the century and are now sought (especially the flat tops) as unique decor — placed beside chairs, in front of couches, and at the foot of beds for extra bedding, and so on. 22½"h x 34"w x 19¾"dp. $185.00.

DOME TOP TRAVEL TRUNK

Pine; iron fixtures and wood-embossed rosettes; can be locked with the original key (a big plus); substantial iron banding; below the lift out tray (its remaining today is another plus) is the usual deep compartment for clothing; the underside of the domed lid is a liner of red embossed tin which was so inexpertly set in, the dealer wondered if it had been added after the trunk's date of origin when a first paper liner became damaged. 18½"h x 28"w x 16"dp. $120.00.

TRAVEL TRUNK
Dated Oct. 4, 1859; reflects the romanticism that the Victorians extended into every phase of their lives. Wood was covered with soft leather, strengthening wood strips and iron bindings added along with brass hardware and leather handles. When found, it contained memorabilia and small clothing items, including a dark silk ruffle-edged parasol. The maker's tag, still very legible, reads: "Made by P & K L Brown, No. 245 Main Street, Worcester, Mass. ...Valise and Carpet Bag Mfgers...Solid leather, fancy, packing, and common...and Ladies' Bonnets and Dress Trunks, Valises, and Bags constantly at hand. Keys fitted — and repairing done at short notice."

The domed lid has two recessed storage compartments, each with a cover lifted by a leather tab; the trunk's deep well base has two separate lidded lift-out boxes that fit down on side ledges. The whole inside of the trunk was lined in fine quality heavy pale gold paper accented with white and darker outlined patterns. On the paper are pictures of luxuriously gowned ladies, modishly garbed men, and scenic backgrounds. (It is said that dolls were often used as the models in order to achieve such facial and finger perfection.)

Carried in the trunk seems to have been "dressy" apparel worn by a young lady of those mid-century years; this silk center-boned-and-laced (vest-like) garment with short capped sleevelets was worn over a balloon-sleeved wide collared waist (today's blouse), the points tightly laced about the mid-section by the long ties, under yards and yards of a skirt long enough that no ankles could be shockingly visible. $650.00.

FOR FUN AND TRANSPORTATION

VICTORIANS
Ca. late 1800's; Alabama residents posing in front of their home for a local photographer. Suitably dressed for an open coach drive to a country picnic with friends soon to be coming by; becoming impatient from waiting (and the slowness of the photography), the gentleman swings between two fingers the heart shaped ornament at the end of his (customarily) gold chain watch fob; his lady has her watch pinned to the bosom of her waist and in one dark silk-gloved hand she waves her palm leaf fan to create a breeze or ward off flying insects. Friends may soon be appearing in a conveyance of the type shown herein.

OPEN COACH
Found in North Carolina; held six riders and a driver; base all original; top has been restored; iron rimmed wooden wheels; dark green with mustard yellow stripping and decoration; buggy whip holder at the side of the driver's seat; used for picnics and other outings for a small group, all sorts of occasions. $895.00.

SLEIGH

Seen in northwestern New York state; described as a vehicle for carrying goods or people on ice and snow; wood, iron, and what was a tufted back leather seat; bowed sides, painted dark with red and yellow trims; ornamental side step and wooden buggy whip holder; the curved front allows riders to stretch out their legs while protecting them from road particles thrown up by horse's hooves; also allowed space to tuck in a heavy robe; the sleigh can be restored; shafts for harnessing are available but not attached. $975.00.

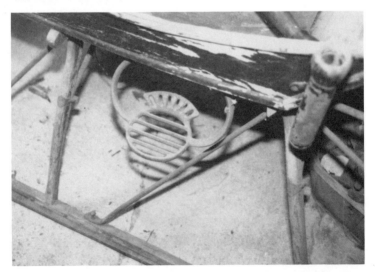

BUGGY/TWO SEATER

Four iron-rimmed wooden wheels; button-back horsehair stuffed plush seat; a plush carriage robe lies on the seat; bowed sides give more room; black painted iron; wood, and leather; top can be folded flat and back; space for children to stand while leaning arms over the back of the seat, or sitting with legs dangling at the rear — and for carrying packages; the usual fancy cast iron steps at each side; front upright floor curtain protects riders' feet and legs from dust, mud, and flying pebbles thrown up by horse's hooves. Horse-drawn transportation has been used through the ages. In larger cities into the 1870's, congestion became so prevalent that police restrictions evolved. Elaborate models were made for the elite "Carriage Trade"; there were livery stables renting "rigs," carriage repair shops everywhere, and plain and patterned cast iron hitching posts (often beside two or three mounting steps) at homes and buildings almost without any exceptions. Before the Civil War most vehicles were custom made in small shops, but after the War "assembly-line" methods were adopted. At one of the centers, Saint Paris in Ohio, partners conceived the idea of making a carriage (or Phaeton) pulled by ponies for children to drive...and after successfully accomplishing their objective, shipping their wagons even to foreign dignitaries everywhere, the name "Pony Wagon Town" was recognized. Truly these conveyances are part of our Victorian heritage...furniture for getting around in. $1,100.00.

GLOSSARY

ACANTHUS — decorative feature adapted in antiquity from the ragged leaves of the prickly acanthus plant native to Europe's Mediterranean regions, and continued through the centuries in decorating on furniture.

ANTIMACASSAR — a cover or tidy to protect the back and arms on chairs, sofas, etc. from hair oils (name originating with popular Antimacassar Oil).

APRON — skirt used as a structural and/or trim aid; designed or plain cut-edged wood strip at the base of cabinet forms, seats, and such; could be metal.

ARMOIRE — a large clothes cupboard first used in the Middle Ages for storing armor and suits of mail.

BELLFLOWER — early motif carved or inlaid of 3 to 5 pointed petals on furniture decorating; adapted from the flower.

BERGÉRE — From Louis XV designers, closed upholstered sides of a loose seat armchair.

BIRDSEYE MAPLE — maple wood having spots resembling birds' eyes — from the buds of boughs driven back into the tree by extremely rough weather.

BOMBÉ — outward swelling; bulbous lines of furniture front and sides.

BRACKET FEET — support corners for a cased piece, triangular with mitered corners, plain or scrolled free sides.

BUHL — earlier called BOULLE after Andre-Charles Boulle, a French designer, 1700's, created beautiful marquetry, as metal, veneer, tortoise shell, and such, popular in furniture inlays.

BUN FOOT — bun shaped flattened ball with a slim ankle.

BURL — an abnormal growth taken from walnut, mahogany, ash, and maple trees with a marbleized or mottled grain, thinly sliced and used on veneers, indicates fine quality furniture.

CABRIOLE LEG — bowlegged — reverse curved leg — where outline is formed from an elongated S-curve; (legs can be the most distinguishing feature of a table and so aid identification); used as early as the 1600's into the 1800's with many variations.

CASED — square box-like enclosing structure — the outside of large items enclosing chests, bureaus, buffets, cabinets, and such.

CHAMFER — corner or edge trimmed to make a slanting surface.

CHALCEDONY — a translucent variety of quartz; a wax-like luster of usually pale blue or gray.

CHEVAL GLASS — full length swinging mirror.

CHIFFONIER — a high, narrow bureau (dresser) with drawers, shelves, and/or cupboard.

CORNICE — horizontal overhanging member of a furniture top.

CROCKET — ornament on furniture resembling carved foliage protruding from a gable or spire, etc.; important in gothic detailing.

CUSP — a pointed end or arch formed by converging curves.

CYMA CURVE — S-shaped wave or curve.

DENTILS — a small rectangular block, as under a cornice, for instance, in a projecting series — like teeth.

DOVETAILED — Joints made by wedge-shaped pieces cut resembling the tail of a dove.

EBONIZED — stained black to simulate ebony.

EMBELLISH — beautify by ornamentation; to create and extend interest in a piece of furniture.

ESCUTCHEON — wood or brass inset or applied fitting around a keyhole.

FINIALS — a terminal piece, usually ornate; turned, cast, or carved.

FLUTING — flat surface grooving or channeling; opposite of reeding.

FRETWORK — perforated, interlaced ornamental work (jigsaw cut) often applied onto solid backgrounds.

GALLERY — practical railing, solid or decorative low upright around tops of furniture forms.

GEOMETRIC — squares, triangles, circles — all interlacing in patterns.

GIMP — narrow fancy fabric trims — usually the edging.

INCISE — ornaments cut deeply into the surface of wood.

INLAY — designs formed on furniture by insertion of contrasting textures, grains, materials, flush with the surface.

KNEES — leg join, ornamental additions to furniture.

KNURL — scrolled addition to furniture decor.

MARQUETRY — decorations colored and flat inlaid in a thin wood veneer surface then glued to furniture, patterns of various woods, bone, ivory, tortoise shell, metals, etc.

MARRIAGE — a piece of good material left on one damaged piece of furniture combined with the usable part of another obsolete item — the two combined to make one good object...also termed "married off."

MOLDING — shaped — ornamental — strips of wood either made or applied on furniture.

MORTISE (and TENON) — joining wood together, the mortise the holes into which the tenons fit — tenons the projections.

MOSQUE — in furniture the tops form of Islamic places of worship.

NACRE — mother of pearl; furniture decor.

ORMOLU — for furniture decorations and mounts, the various copper, tin and zinc alloys that are like gold in appearance.

PEDIMENT — molded or other ornamental structures atop cased furniture.

BROKEN PEDIMENT — a pediment interrupted with a separate crest at its highest peak.

RANDOM WIDTH — whatever boards are available (as leftovers usually) to form inconspicuous parts of furniture pieces — width not important — for the backs of cupboards, and such.

ROUNDEL — a furniture term for round or circular ornaments.

REEDING — the opposite of fluting — a series of small, parallel ridges.

RUG CUTTER — chair rockers so narrow they were making impressions deep in carpeting.

SERPENTINE CURVE — case pieces fronts having waving curves.

SLAT — chairback horizontal crossbars; the wood pieces which fit between siderails of a bed to hold the tier above — earlier cornshucks mattresses — later springs.

SPLAT — center upright in the back of chairs, plain or decorative.

SPOOL TURNINGS — a series of connecting ball turnings made to resemble spools of thread.

STILE — upright elements in a frame — as the side supports of a chair back.

STRETCHER — horizontal underside bracings for tables and chairs, plain or decorated.

SPINDLES — decorative turned piece in wood, lathe turned.

VENEER — thin layer of wood or various other materials glued for ornamentation to surfaces of solid woods.

WHORL FOOT — upturned scroll — a knurl

INDEX

Schroeder's
ANTIQUES
Price Guide ... is the #1 best-selling

antiques & collectibles value guide on the market today,
and here's why . . .

Schroeder's
ANTIQUES
Price Guide

OUR **1** *BEST SELLER!*

Identification & Values Of Over 50,000 Antiques & Collectibles

8½ X 11 • 608 Pgs. • PB • $12.95

• *More than 300 advisors, well-known dealers, and top-notch collectors work together with our editors to bring you accurate information regarding pricing and identification.*

• *More than 45,000 items in almost 500 categories are listed along with hundreds of sharp original photos that illustrate not only the rare and unusual, but the common, popular collectibles as well.*

• *Each large close-up shot shows important details clearly. Every subject is represented with histories and background information, a feature not found in any of our competitors' publications.*

• *Our editors keep abreast of newly-developing trends, often adding several new categories a year as the need arises.*

If it merits the interest of today's collector, you'll find it in *Schroeder's*. And you can feel confident that the information we publish is up to date and accurate. Our advisors thoroughly check each category to spot inconsistencies, listings that may not be entirely reflective of market dealings, and lines too vague to be of merit. Only the best of the lot remains for publication.

Without doubt, you'll find
**SCHROEDER'S ANTIQUES
PRICE GUIDE**
the only one to buy for
reliable information and values.

COLLECTOR BOOKS
A Division of Schroeder Publishing Co., Inc.